SHORT WALKS FROM

Suffolk Pubs

Jean and Geoff Pratt

COUNTRYSIDE BOOKS
NEWBURY, BERKSHIRE

COUNTRYSIDE BOOKS
3 Catherine Road
Newbury, Berkshire

ISBN 1 85306 341 X

Designed by Mon Mohan
Cover illustration by Colin Doggett
Photographs and maps by the authors

Produced through MRM Associates Ltd., Reading
Typeset by Acorn Bookwork, Salisbury
Printed by Woolnough Ltd., Irthlingborough, Northants.

Contents

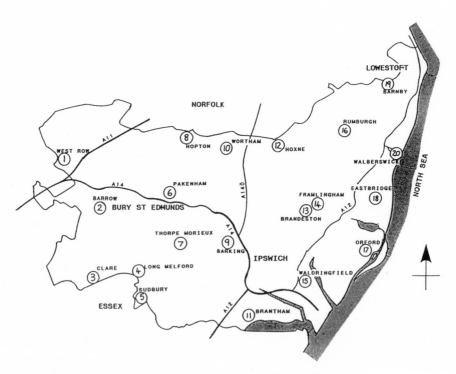

Area map showing the locations of the walks.

Introduction

Throughout past ages men and women have walked and ridden from farm to farm and from village to village across the countryside, and in so doing they have trodden out the vast number of footpaths and bridleways which now form the countrywide network of rights of way.

The heritage of footpaths and bridleways enables us all to explore and enjoy the local countryside, finding picturesque spots, magnificent views and interesting wildlife wherever we go, and this is particularly true in Suffolk, which has a wide variety of landscape. Being spread across the county, this selection of 20 short walks will enable users to get to know the range of landscapes which can be found.

Each pub has been chosen as a place where good food can be eaten in comfortable and attractive surroundings, and from where you can start an interesting short circular walk.

On weekdays, pubs may open between 11 am and 11 pm and the actual opening times are at the discretion of the owner or landlord. In practice, however, most pubs are open between 11.30 am and 2.30 pm and again from 6.30 pm to 11 pm. In those cases where a pub is currently open more than 30 minutes earlier or 30 minutes later than these usual times, a comment is made in the description of the pub. On Sundays, the statutory opening times from 12 noon to 3 pm and from 7 pm to 10.30 pm apply.

Meals are usually served between 12 noon and 2.30 pm and between 6.30 pm and 9.30 pm. Here again any significant variation in these hours is mentioned in the text. In general, food is readily available but sometimes there may be a rush of customers. If time is critical or if you are using the pub at a busy season, it is a good idea to telephone.

Nearly all the pubs mentioned in this book welcome children, though most would say that they prefer them seated at tables with adults, while indoors, rather than running around, as staff and customers need to carry food and drink to and from the tables. In general, dogs are not allowed where food is served.

When walking in the country, dogs can be tempted to chase livestock and game birds, with dire consequences for both. The Country Code states that all dogs should be under control, so leads are often advisable.

The sketch maps are intended as a simple guide and are not to scale. Details, such as hedges, ditches and bridges, are shown where they may help to identify the route, but otherwise are omitted. The relevant number in the Ordnance Survey Landranger 1:50 000 series is also given with each walk.

Should you wish to leave a car at a pub whilst taking a walk, it is best to check with the landlord. If parking elsewhere than at a recognised car park, please be careful not to cause an obstruction to local residents. Remember also that most minor roads can be used by very large farm machinery.

All the walks are on public rights of way or permissive paths, or, in one case, across a village green. Although the Suffolk County Council's Rights of Way Officers do their best to ensure that the paths are maintained and kept usable, the condition of rural footpaths and bridleways can vary greatly, depending on the amount and type of usage, the recent weather conditions and the season. In summer natural vegetation may grow quickly and tend to obscure the way, and paths can be illegally obstructed by growing crops. In winter any path may become muddy and puddly, consequently stout footwear is always advisable.

The help given by the Suffolk County Council's Rights of Way staff is appreciated.

Finally, we hope that with this book and the Ordnance Survey map, you will enjoy your forays into the Suffolk countryside, and be encouraged to explore more of our lovely county.

Jean and Geoff Pratt
Spring 1995

Publisher's Note

We hope that you obtain considerable enjoyment from this book; great care has been taken in its preparation. However, changes of landlord and actual closures are sadly not uncommon. Likewise, although at the time of publication all routes followed public rights of way or permitted paths, diversion orders can be made and permissions withdrawn.

We cannot of course be held responsible for such diversion orders and any inaccuracies in the text which result from these or any other changes to the routes, nor any damage which might result from walkers trespassing on private property. However, we are anxious that all details covering the walks and the pubs are kept up to date and would therefore welcome information from readers which would be relevant to future editions.

1 West Row
The Jude's Ferry

West Row is at the north-west corner of Suffolk and about 3 miles west of the centre of Mildenhall. This area is quite different from other parts of Suffolk, because it lies right at the edge of the Cambridgeshire Fens, on rich black peaty soil, a mere 15 ft above sea level. To the south of the village, the river Lark flows westwards from its source near Bury St Edmunds to the river Great Ouse, near Ely.

The Jude's Ferry is a spacious, comfortable riverside pub where a large open wood fire burns in the grate when days get chilly. The original owner, Jude, used to ferry travellers across the river in the days before the nearby bridge was built. In the 1900s the river here was frequently used for baptisms. The pub is actually a timber-framed house, but in 1849 it was given a skin of Suffolk white bricks. High in the gable on the road frontage of the pub is a plaque saying 'WH 1849'. The large garden, with a long, idyllic river frontage onto the river Lark, is set with benches and tables under the willows. A separate garden with children's play apparatus will keep the young ones happy. Sheep graze in an adjacent field, which will interest most children, watching over the fence. Well-behaved dogs are welcome.

The wide-ranging menu covers fresh salmon steak, grilled rainbow trout with crabmeat and almond topping, smoked salmon and prawns, steak and mushrooms cooked in beer with shortcrust pastry, southern fried chicken, vegetable lasagne, chilli bean pasty, nut and mushroom bake and grilled chicken butterfly breast with mushrooms. A selection of sweets is available from the trolley. Children sitting at tables, eating with their parents, are welcome. They may have either small portions from the main menu or choose from the children's specials, such as hamburgers, hot dogs or pizza with chips, plus ice-cream. The spectrum of real ales includes Adnams Best and Broadside, Bass, Hancock's HB, with regular guests like Wadworth 6X, Young's Special and Old Speckled Hen. Draught ciders on offer are Taunton Dry Blackthorn or Sweet. The pub is open during the usual hours and food is available at all times.

Telephone: 01638 712277.

How to get there: From the Barton Mills roundabout on the A11 (Newmarket to Norwich Road) follow the A1101 to Mildenhall. In the centre of the town take the minor road towards West Row and in 1½ miles turn left and then left again on the road to Freckenham. The Jude's Ferry is on the far side of the village by the bridge over the river Lark.

Parking: The pub car park is large. If you would like to leave the car there while you walk be sure to ask the landlord first.

Length of the walk: 3½ miles (a short cut saving 1 mile is possible). Map: OS Landranger sheet 143 Ely, Wisbech and surrounding area (inn GR 677749).

This walks starts along the north bank of the meandering river Lark upstream of Jude's Ferry Bridge. The middle section of the route is over farm paths and tracks and through the village, passing the church, back to the river. The walk returns to the inn along the river bank.

The Walk
From the inn go down the road to the Jude's Ferry Bridge. Just at the edge of the bridge turn left, over a stile, and descend the steps to the river bank. Follow the path upstream beside the river Lark, passing a farm on the left and later, on the opposite side of the river, a concrete World War II 'pill box'.

The path runs beside trees which line the north bank. The river swings round in a gentle curve to the right and here there are trees on both sides of the river. Shortly after, the river makes a sharp turn to the left, and the trees both sides end within sight of a large riverside house, called Kings Staunch Cottage, where there is a weir across the river.

Keep on the riverside path and, at a kissing-gate leading into the garden, turn left beside a laurel hedge and follow the hedge for 100 yards to a grassy cart track and turn left.

8

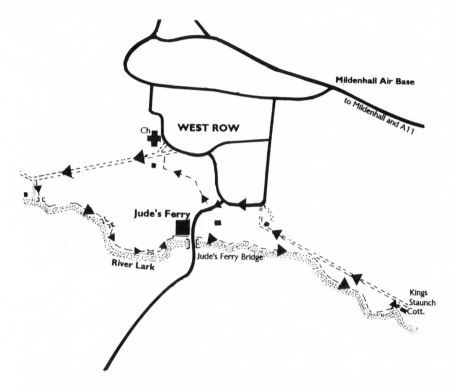

Walk the cart track. Way beyond the field on the right, you can see the buildings of the busy Mildenhall Air Base, which, with its 2-mile long runway, is capable of accommodating the largest aircraft. In about ½ mile go straight past a cottage on the right and, where the hedge on the right ends, go right along a cross-field path to meet Bargate Road at a right angle bend and turn left. Pass Neve Gardens on the right and after Bargate Lane on the left, go left down Ferry Lane, signposted 'Isleham and Freckenham'.

For a short cut back to the Jude's Ferry, keep on this road for 300 yards.

To continue the walk, go down Ferry Lane for 100 yards and go right immediately after No 136, Feltwell House, on a wide grass path alongside the back gardens of bungalows on the right. At a junction of paths go slightly left and continue, following the field boundary. Come to a point about 100 yards before the white farmhouse of Popes Farm, and here turn right on a narrow grass path, passing a plantation of young conifers on the right.

This path leads out to a road junction beside the church and a small green on which the war memorial and village sign stand. Go left, along Church Lane, and soon pass an attractive white building on the left and

9

Kings Staunch Cottage, beside the river Lark.

Pamment's Lane also on the left. Shortly after, the road, now a narrow lane between hedges, is called The Gravel.

In just over ¼ mile, and before reaching an isolated bungalow on the left, the track comes out to a wider grass verge and crosses a deep drainage ditch. Here turn left at a footpath sign, along a headland path with the deep ditch on the right. At the corner of the field cross a bridge over a ditch and continue by following the river Lark on the right.

Keep to the river bank for almost a mile, crossing en route several stiles, a pair of bridges in quick succession and a longer bridge leading into a riverside meadow. Go over another stile beside a mooring, then turn left along a waymarked path which leads into the car park of the Jude's Ferry.

Barrow
The Weeping Willow

Barrow is a picturesque village with a green and a village sign at the centre, and, beside the road out to Higham, a large duck pond. To the north, there are wide views of a landscape of gently sloping fields and hedges dotted with mature trees. However, interesting changes are occurring because of the extensive planting of new hardwood trees. Opposite the pub is a strange looking tower. On that site once stood a Salvation Army citadel. When the citadel became redundant it was to be sold and it is said that a loyal member, fearing it might be used for dancing or bingo, bought it and demolished it, all save the tower. What might be thought to be buttresses are in fact the remains of the side walls.

The Weeping Willow has two quite separate bars. The comfortable lounge bar has an enormous fireplace, with two corresponding deep inglenooks on either side. Some of the many old black beams are a bit awry by today's standards. The other, larger, bar has a pool table in a side area. Children are welcome – they have their own menu, and a high chair is available. In the pleasant garden, with the weeping willow tree, there is plenty of room to run around, and swings to enjoy. In summer a bouncy castle will amuse the younger ones.

On the menu are mainly home-made dishes, such as cheese and mushroom pancakes, avocado and corn bake, chicken tikka masala, lasagne verdi, golden seafood platter, deep-fried cod fillet, thick omelettes, steak and kidney pie, quarter of a roast chicken, 8 oz sirloin steak and more. Among the sweets on offer are banana split, mint cooler, treacle pudding and ice-creams. On Sundays you can have a traditional Sunday lunch. The real ales served are Greene King IPA, Bitter, Abbot and XX Mild. Dry Blackthorn draught cider is on sale. The pub is open at the usual times for both food and drink at lunchtimes and in the evenings every day. It stays open till 3.30 in the afternoon. Dogs are not allowed inside, with the exception of guide dogs of course.

Telephone: 01284 810492.

How to get there: Barrow lies between Newmarket and Bury St Edmunds. From Newmarket, take the first slip road from the A14 after passing the Kentford Service Area, or, from Bury, take the third slip road after the A134 and A143 grade-separated junction by the sugar beet factory silos. From the A14, go south for 2 miles and at the Barrow village green turn left to the Weeping Willow.

Parking: The car park at the Weeping Willow is quite large. It is also possible to park beside the road in the village.

Length of the walk: 3 miles (or 2½ if the church is missed out). Map: OS Landranger sheet 155 Bury St Edmunds and Sudbury area (inn GR 766635).

This easy walk circles the northern side of the village, going at first along a well-used grassy headland path to Barrow church. After retracing the way a little, the walk takes a cross-field path and then skirts an interesting man-made lake and, after a short walk along a minor road, returns, via a good track, to the Weeping Willow. There are fine views along the route.

The Walk

From the Weeping Willow go left to the green and, almost opposite the prominent village sign, turn right on a narrow footpath beside a flint-faced wall, which leads towards Barrow church. After passing some bungalows on the right, meet and cross Ley Road. Continue straight over, along a tarmac garage forecourt and a short green lane, to the entrance to a playing field.

Do not enter the playing field but keep straight on along a broad, grassy headland path, with a hedge on the left. Keep to the headland as the path turns half-right at a corner and keep straight on at the next corner into another field. There is a footpath sign here. Continue along the headland, with the hedge on the left.

Soon you come to a point where the headland path crosses a grassy cart track at right angles and then swings slightly left. The walk returns to this

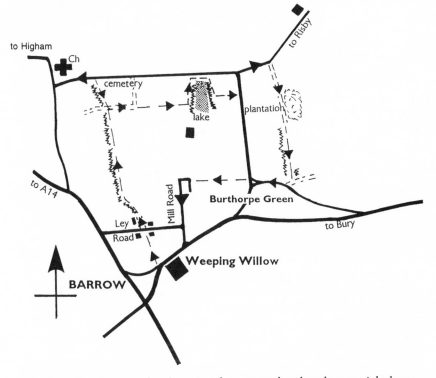

point later, but for any who do not wish to go to the church, turn right here.

If continuing to Barrow church, keep on alongside the headland. At the corner of the field go on a narrow footpath, with a cemetery on the right, and turn left at the road for 200 yards to reach the church. When you are ready to go on with the walk, retrace your steps and turn right along the footpath beside the cemetery. Continue on the headland path for about 100 yards and, leaving the path you were on earlier, go left on the grassy cross-field cart track.

At the far side of the field, where the track goes left at a waymark, keep straight on along a reinstated cross-field footpath, dropping to a hedge in a shallow valley on the opposite side of the field. Swing left at a waymark, on a headland path. Looking through the hedge on the right, you will glimpse a pleasant lake surrounded by a narrow lawn.

Turn right at the corner of the field and go along a narrow path between a roadside hedge on the left and a tall fence, behind which is the earth dam at the end of the lake. On reaching the next corner of the fence, at a waymark, turn right, climbing away from the road, with a fence on the right and beyond it the lake. Pass a plantation of young mixed woodland.

Old Lamb Cottages, Burthorpe Green.

About 100 yards from the corner, swing left on a grass path through the plantation and continue straight along a cross-field footpath. There are good, wide views of the countryside over to the left here. Go down steps and over a sleeper bridge, to a road. Turn left. In 100 yards at a T-junction turn right on the road to Risby. Where the road swings sharp left down towards a massive barn, go right along a cart track, following the overhead electricity poles.

At first there is a field on the left and a ditch on the right but soon there are young trees, mostly oaks, on the left. As you look around you will see many areas of new woodland. Beyond the next field boundary, the track changes to a broad grass headland and at the far side of the field the path becomes a short green lane. In 100 yards, at a footpath sign, go right, out to a road and bear slightly right along it.

When you come to Burthorpe Green, a triangular grass area with roads on all sides, go straight on, passing the Old Lamb and Old Lamb Cottage. At the corner of the green cross the Risby road and follow the wide, grassy footpath straight on towards Barrow Green. Pass on the left an orchard. This path leads into a road at a right angle bend. The road straight ahead is Mill Road and the cul-de-sac on the left is Orchard Way.

Go straight along Mill Road and keep with it as it turns left. Pass Ley Road on the right. Turn right at the T-junction and you will soon reach the Weeping Willow.

Clare
The Bell Hotel

③

Clare's history has been charted since at least the time of the Norman Conquest. When the Domesday Book was compiled there were only six boroughs in Suffolk, of which one was Clare. William the Conqueror gave land here to his cousin, Richard Fitzgilbert, who built the castle on a small hillock beside the Stour. Just across the river is Clare Priory. Belonging to the Augustinian order, it was founded in 1249 and lasted until Henry VIII dissolved the monasteries. In 1953 the Austin friars returned. A feature of many of the old houses in Clare is the pargeting on the walls.

The Bell Hotel, by Market Hill in the centre of Clare, traces its history back to the 16th century and there is, allegedly, a ghost here. This is a comfortable hotel, giving an unhurried atmosphere, though service is prompt! Accommodation is available. The Garden Room, where meals are served and children are welcome, leads onto a terrace. The restaurant is open in the evenings. Outside, there is a garden area.

On the interesting menu are pasta carbonara, battered seafood, lamb cutlets with sauté potatoes, crispy aromatic duckling, marinated pork and beef stir-fry with hoisin sauce, chilli chicken and braised Growler beef – Old Growler being an ale brewed locally at the Nethergate Brewery. Desserts can be chosen from chocolate mousse with edible flowers, apple and cherry crumble, ice-cream in a brandysnap basket and hot toffee bananas with banana ice-cream. A menu for 'the little people' lists sausage and mash, chicken nuggets and chips, fishy fingers with baked beans and turkey dinosaurs. High chairs are provided. The real ales served are Nethergate and Greene King IPA. Stowford draught cider is also available. The hotel is open 7 days a week and meals can be provided each day at lunchtime and in the evenings. Well-behaved dogs are welcome.

Telephone: 01787 277741.

How to get there: Take the A134 road between Sudbury and Bury. Turn off to the west onto the A1092 at a junction just north of Long Melford. Clare is reached in 6 miles. The Bell Hotel is on the main road, Market Hill, opposite the war memorial.

Parking: There is a large car park at the Clare Country Park, which is within easy reach of the Bell Hotel. On Market Hill, opposite the Bell, public parking is available, except on Mondays and Saturdays. A certain amount of kerbside parking can be found around the town. At the Bell, parking is very limited.

Length of the walk: 3 miles (short cut available). Map: OS Landranger sheet 155 Bury St Edmunds and Sudbury area (inn GR 770453).

The castle, its environs, and the site of the former railway station form the Clare Country Park. You can explore the ruined keep and the remains of the castle walls, or wander beside the tranquil river Stour and join the nature trail. In one corner of the country park is a children's play area.

The walk starts by going through the country park and then along the bank of the Stour to the site of a former mill. It continues northward beside a shallow valley on a well-walked path to Hermitage Farm, and then across Clare Common, the site of an Iron Age fort over 2,000 years old, where you can still see some remains of ditches and ramparts as a reminder of the past. The return is over well-used field paths to the river Stour and then along the river bank for a short distance back to the town.

The Walk
Go left from the Bell Hotel and in 100 yards turn left down Station Road. At the end enter Clare Country Park. Keep on the tarmac drive and soon reach the old station building, once serving the former railway line along the Stour valley.

Turn right and go to the left of the goods shed and the car park, where you will come to the river Stour. Follow the river bank for a few yards and then cross the river by the old railway bridge.

Immediately beyond the bridge turn sharp left through a pedestrian gate

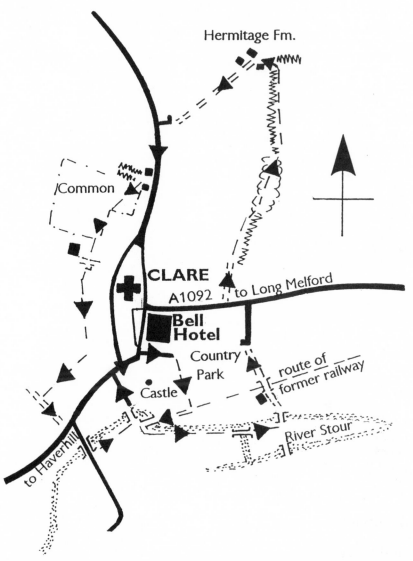

along a footpath beside the river. Cross a bridge over a weir where the main flow of the river goes right. Keep straight on beside a fence on the left. Beyond the fence is a narrow branch of the river which at one time fed a watermill.

Just before an old brick barn go left through a tall steel kissing-gate and cross a concrete slab bridge. Pass the restored Mill House on the left and

17

Clare Priory

continue up the lane, over a bridge crossing the former railway cutting, along which runs a footpath in the country park. When the lane joins a road, go straight on along it. In about 200 yards join the A1092 at a T-junction. Go left for 100 yards and turn right at a footpath sign along Eastfield Farm Road.

The tarmac track leads past a sports field on the left and ends just beyond a large house. Keep on a cart track close to the hedge on the right. You are on the Stour Valley Way. Pass a farm on the left and, still beside the hedge, keep along a grass path which leads into a narrow path between trees. Soon this becomes a pleasant green lane which eventually swings right to a stile leading into a large field. Turn left along the headland.

At the field corner, where the Stour Valley Path turns right, go half-left through the hedge close to a twin electricity pole. Keep the barn on the left, and at a waymark turn left along a farm drive, passing barns and the white-painted Hermitage Farm on the right. Follow the farm drive for about ¼ mile to join Hermitage Meadow, an estate road, at a bend. Keep straight on for a further 100 yards and turn left.

Walk down the main road towards Clare for about 200 yards and just before the 30 mph sign turn right beside a black weatherboarded lean-to building along a wide, well-used grass path. In 100 yards leave the path and turn left over a stile onto Clare Common. Make for the right-hand end of a brick boundary wall seen ahead.

When you reach the end of the brick wall, at the corner of the common, go left beside the boundary fence. Drop down to cross a cart track and keep straight on, but bear slightly away from the fence on the left and ignore the kissing-gate. When you reach a hedge go over a stile beside a small pond and along a narrow footpath, with a school behind a fence on the right.

On reaching the entrance to the school, cross the road and take a narrow path, which snakes right and left, between cupressus trees. In 100 yards enter the cemetery and keep straight on. At the next field, drop down a small bank and follow the headland path beside a high flint and brick wall on the left. At the corner, turn right at a waymark.

For a short cut back to the town and the start, turn left here.

For the main walk, keep on the headland, still following a brick and flint wall which is punctuated by delightful little arched gateways. Pass a black weatherboarded house beside the wall and keep straight on. Reach a large field and turn left along a cart track leading directly to a road. Turn left for a few yards and then right, along Ashen Road. Cross the river, then immediately turn left, and walk beside the water on the left. On the right is the shallow embankment of the disused railway.

You will soon come to a footbridge across the river. Nearby on the right, beyond the former railway, is a narrow gate which leads to the priory. Cross the footbridge, and go straight on along the road to a T-junction. Turn right along the main road, pass High Street on the left and then swing left into Market Hill and back to the Bell.

④ Long Melford
The Cock and Bell

Long Melford is an attractive village with a wide main street, flanked with a mixture of houses, shops, and inns, most of which are old. The street is about a mile long and this has given the village its appellation 'Long'. At the north end is Melford Green, a broad finger of open grassland stretching ½ mile up to Holy Trinity church and bordered on one side by Elizabethan Melford Hall. Surprisingly, Long Melford has another large historic mansion within the parish, Kentwell Hall, a brick-built moated manor house of similar age. This is a popular tourist area, with much to see.

The Cock and Bell, fronting Hall Street, has been a pub for 400 years or so. It was a 16th century coaching inn on the route from Bury St Edmunds to Sudbury, and still offers accommodation. Many a cock fight has taken place here. The slightly sunken area you will notice to the right of the front door was the pit. Around the walls are framed illustrations of some of the paraphernalia of those long-gone days – the number of different types of spurs is staggering. Pity those poor birds. The long bar, across the frontage, has retained the original beams. Beyond the bar is a restaurant for evening meals.

Much of the food is home-cooked. You will find Spanish omelette, spinach and ricotta cannelloni, grilled fillet of plaice, Yorkshire pudding filled with braised steak and many traditional country pies – chicken and leek, lamb and apricot, pork and cider, steak and ale. Also on offer are roast pheasant and roast pork, and seven different ploughman's lunches. Bakewell tart, treacle tart, baked apple and apple flan are among the delicious home-made desserts. The real ales served are Directors, Ruddles, John Smith's and a guest ale which changes weekly. Scrumpy Jack is the draught cider on sale. The Cock and Bell is open all day on Monday to Saturday, and all the permitted hours on Sunday. Meals are served lunchtimes and evenings seven days a week. Well-behaved children are welcome, they may dine in the restaurant or in the area known as The Pit. A high chair is available. Dogs, if well-trained, are also welcome.

Telephone: 01787 379807.

How to get there: Long Melford is about 3 miles north of Sudbury. Take the A134 Sudbury to Bury St Edmunds road. The main road bypasses the village, so follow the signs to Long Melford. The Cock and Bell is on the west side of the main street.

Parking: At the rear of the pub is a large car park. The main street is wide and cars can be parked there.

Length of the walk: 2½ miles. Map: OS Landranger sheet 155 Bury St Edmunds and Sudbury area (inn GR 863456).

From the Cock and Bell, the walk follows the main street, crossing the Chad Brook, to Melford Green. It passes the wall of Melford Hall (National Trust) and continues to the top of the village and along the lime-tree avenue towards Kentwell Hall. The return is across a field to Long Melford church – a visit is recommended – and on cross-field paths and lanes back to the pub.

The Walk

From the Cock and Bell go left along the main village street. At the pelican crossing cross the road and continue in the same direction as before. Pass the Bull, another old coaching inn, on the right and Brook House, a timber and brick dwelling dated 1610, almost opposite. Cross a side road, leave the roadside footway and keep straight on beside houses on the right with the village sign on a wide, grass verge on the left. The path leads to a narrow pedestrian bridge over Chad Brook.

Beyond the bridge you reach Long Melford Green. Keep on along the edge, with a moat and the wall of Melford Hall on the right. Overtopping the wall is the large brick summerhouse-cum-gazebo which at one time was used by Beatrix Potter, who often visited the Hall, where her cousin lived. In one room of the house is a collection of Beatrix Potter memorabilia. Jeremy Fisher was dreamt up by a pond here.

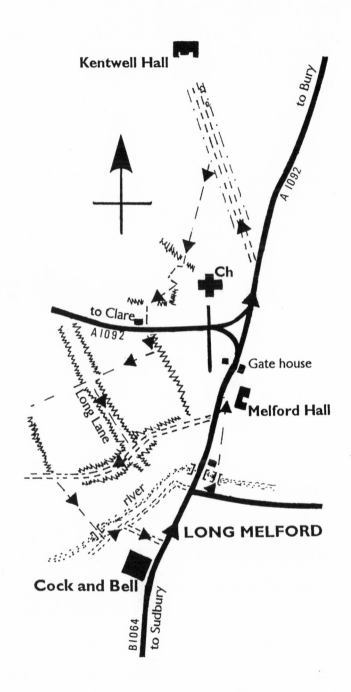

Kentwell Hall

to Bury

A 1092

Ch

to Clare

A 1092

Gate house

Long Lane

Melford Hall

river

LONG MELFORD

Cock and Bell

B 1064

to Sudbury

Entrance gateway to Melford Hall.

At the Hall's impressive brick gatehouse cross the road. Keep on the footway beside the road and continue northward to the end of the Green, and then go a further 100 yards along the road. Bear left, off the road, on the long, straight lime avenue towards Kentwell Hall, seen in the distance.

About halfway to Kentwell, and some 10 yards before a corner of the field on the left, go over an iron stile with a wooden footpiece, in the fence on the left.

Before leaving the drive, if you have time, you could walk further along it, maybe as far as the point where the public footpath leaves the drive, just before the entrance gates, to go round to the side of the Hall, and then return to the stile.

Having crossed the stile go half-left towards a point slightly right of Long Melford church tower. Cross the pasture and go over a two-step stile, through a narrow wood and out by another stile into a small paddock. On the far side cross a stile and turn left for 50 yards to the corner of the field.

At this point you are close to Holy Trinity, a large, magnificent church built in the late 15th century.

Leaving the church, from the footpath sign at the edge of the field take a diagonal path across the corner of the field to a gap in the hedge on the south side, about 200 yards away. At the gap go over a stile without a footpiece, into a grass field, on the far side of which is a very large bungalow, with a clock in the gable facing you. Go towards the left-hand side of the building, and cross a stile in the ranch-type fencing about 10 yards from the corner of the bungalow. Pass through a narrow way cut through a thick cupressus hedge, over a low wall to a road.

Cross the road and, almost opposite, take a headland path, with a hedge on the left. In about 100 yards, at a waymark, turn right along a cross-field path, almost along a line of electricity poles. At the far side of the field turn left at a waymark, down a narrow permissive footpath between hedges. In about 300 yards meet a green lane at right angles and turn right along it.

About 50 yards beyond where the hedges beside the track end, turn left on a narrow field-edge path leading towards buildings in Long Melford, and passing close to an electricity pole. Go beside an allotment, over a foot-bridge across a stream and at a T-junction of paths go left on a well-used track.

When you reach the end of Cock and Bell Lane, a narrow tarmac road with terraced houses both sides, turn right. Pass a crinkle-crankle wall and at the main road turn right to the pub, about 20 yards away.

Places of interest nearby

Melford Hall (National Trust). This Tudor brick mansion, with many turrets, was built around 1600. It is open in April on Saturdays, Sundays and bank holiday Mondays, and from May through to September on Wednesdays, Thursdays, Saturdays and Sundays and bank holiday Mondays. In October it is only open on Saturdays and Sundays. The opening times are always 2 pm to 5.30 pm. Telephone: 01787 880286. *Kentwell Hall* is sometimes open to the public, mainly on Sundays and around school holiday times, but not in winter. It is known for its open days when, for a short season, people in period costume inhabit the rooms and environs of the Hall, re-enacting the social, domestic and working life of a great historic estate. Telephone: 01787 310217.

⑤ Sudbury
The Boathouse Hotel

Sudbury is an old, well-established town, having a Royal Charter in 1559. At one time it was a centre for weaving and there are many examples of weavers' cottages to be seen. Now it is a busy market town with several factories. A strongly flowing river is a source of power and the Stour has been harnessed to drive several watermills in the neighbourhood. Across the watermeadows there are dams, sluices and channels which convey the water to the mills.

The Boathouse Hotel is on the edge of Sudbury and faces the river. From the restaurant, bars and the riverside garden, one can see the boats going up and down, or watch fishermen patiently waiting a tug on their lines. The comfortable bars make one feel in no hurry to leave. The main bar is subdivided into three smaller areas, giving a homely air. Down some stairs just off the bar is a games room. On summer Sundays barbecues are held in the large garden. Accommodation is available, also with river views. In summer rowing boats can be hired from the hotel and, with a permit (free to residents), you may fish from the river frontage. A 26 lb carp is the record to date.

The food is good and plentiful. On the menu are Barnsley lamb chops with blackberry and apricot sauce, sizzling chicken, Cajun-style, beef and

25

coconut curry, sweet and sour pork, lamb korma and beef in brown ale. Besides the home-made pudding of the day there is steamed chocolate pudding, banana fudge cake, traditional treacle sponge and ginger in cream and meringue baskets. On summer Sundays cream teas can be obtained – delicious. The real ales served include Old Growler, a local brew from nearby Clare, Greene King IPA, Adnams Best Bitter and one guest ale. Scrumpy Jack and Strongbow draught cider are on sale. Children are well catered for. They have their own menu, and may eat in either of the areas away from the bar. They will enjoy the garden, but as it is alongside the river supervision is necessary. Dogs are welcome, if well-behaved.

The summer opening times, April to September, are from 11 am to 3 pm and 5.30 pm to 11 pm on Mondays to Fridays, all day on Saturdays and the permitted hours on Sundays. Meals are served at the usual times, except that no food is available on Sundays. In winter, the hotel is closed at Monday lunchtimes.

Telephone: 01787 379090.

How to get there: Sudbury is in the south-west of Suffolk, close by the Essex border. To get to the Boathouse Hotel, travel round the Sudbury town centre one-way gyratory system and take the A131, south-west towards Halstead. The hotel is on the right immediately before Ballingdon Bridge, which crosses the river Stour.

Parking: There is limited parking at the Boathouse Hotel. However, there is the Valley Walk car park 200 yards away across Ballingdon Bridge, on the right just by a disused railway bridge over the road. There are also several car parks in and around Sudbury town centre.

Length of the walk: 2 miles. Map: OS Landranger sheet 155 Bury St Edmunds and Sudbury area (inn GR 868409).

This short and pleasant walk starts by Ballingdon Bridge, and soon enters the Commons, the watermeadows beside the river Stour which have belonged to the people of Sudbury for generations. At first the route follows the tail race from the former Sudbury Mill. This prominent white building is now a hotel, but it still has the mill stream running beneath the building and has preserved the old water wheel. After passing the mill the walk continues beside the river, going by a large weir to reach the settlement of Brundon and the picturesque Brundon Mill, now converted into dwellings. The return is along the Valley Walk, a permissive path on a former railway track, partly in cutting and partly on the embankment.

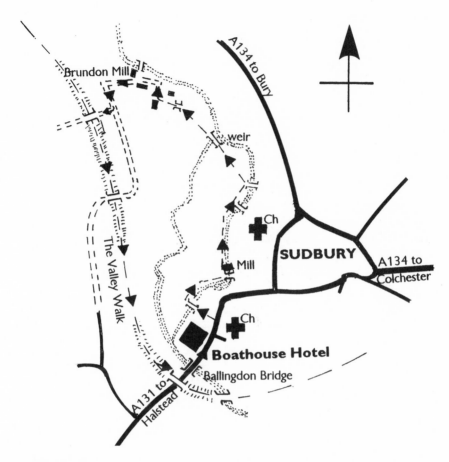

The Walk

From the Boathouse Hotel turn left and, after passing Church Street on the right, turn left down Noah's Ark Lane, a narrow alley, which leads to a little footpath between walls and then across a concrete bridge over the former mill race, onto the meadow known as Freeman's Little Common.

Turn right beside the stream, opposite which are high walls enclosing rear gardens and two interesting conical-shaped gazebos almost standing in the stream itself.

Follow the stream round to the right by some willow trees, crossing a small ditch by a wide culvert and then going directly towards the Mill Hotel. Go through an iron kissing-gate, and immediately turn left beside the hotel. If you look through the broad picture window you may glimpse the old mill wheel, encased in glass in the hotel lounge, proudly demonstrating its his-

Brundon Mill.

toric past. In a wall inside, behind a glass panel, is a mummified cat, another relic of the past. There was once a custom of entombing a live cat in the walls of a building when it was built, for good luck (or against evil spirits).

Keep on the gravel path beside the mill stream. After passing a small children's play area and paddling pool on the left, reach a broad footbridge leading to the Croft and St Gregory's church.

Continue along the path beside the river. Do not cross the next concrete bridge but go straight through a squeezer stile then bear half-left across Sudbury Common Lands Nature Reserve towards a Second World War fortification (a 'pill box') beyond a wooden fence on the far side of the field. On the right beside the river you can see some steps – this was an Edwardian bathing place.

Go through a gate leading to a concrete footbridge. On the right there is a broad weir, on the right-hand side of which are a series of five small pools forming a fish ladder by which fish, such as salmon, may at one time have made their way upstream beside the weir and a waterfall.

Keep straight on along a broad, grassy path, passing the pill box on the right. Cross a timber footbridge and a stile and then continue parallel to the hedge on the right, towards a cottage and a tall brick wall. Leave the meadow by a stile beside a brick wall on the right, onto a gravel track. In about 100 yards swing left beside a row of weatherboarded cottages, with the lovely Brundon Mill ahead.

Do not turn in front of the mill but take the gravel track half-left, keeping the mill building on the right. In 100 yards the track bends sharply left. Pass a house and a farmyard on the left. Immediately beyond the brick barn, go right on a gravel road between hedges, climbing up an embankment to cross the former railway.

Immediately before the bridge go left on a narrow path along the top of the embankment for 75 yards and then descend steps to reach the Valley Walk. Turn left along the cutting. Soon after going under a brick arch bridge the path leaves the cutting and runs along the embankment. On the left are the meadows and beyond is St Gregory's church. Pass Sudbury Wanderers Football Club ground on the right.

You will cross a steel girder bridge over a narrow drainage ditch, and All Saints church is seen on your left. Shortly after, leave the Valley Walk and go left on a wide track down the embankment to a car park. Bear right out to the road, and turn left along Ballingdon Road. Cross Ballingdon Bridge back to the Boathouse.

Places of interest nearby

Gainsborough's House, a museum and art gallery, is in Gainsborough Street. The painter, Gainsborough, was born in Sudbury.

⑥ Pakenham
The Fox

Pakenham nestles beside a small stream which flows northward for a mile to join the river, Black Bourn, just at the edge of Ixworth. On either side of the stream there is a strip of low-lying ground beyond which the land rises to a broad plateau. The houses which make up the village street are of a variety of ages and styles. In spite of the differences, every building seems to have been fitted to its neighbour and there is a unified appearance – and some lovely gardens.

The Fox is a typical, old country inn. It is believed to be one of the first of the Greene King pubs. Their brewery in nearby Bury St Edmunds dates from 1799. The Greene family used to live in Pakenham at Nether Hall, which is only ¼ mile to the south. Their farm labourers walked over the fields at lunchtimes to eat their sandwiches, and to read their newspapers, in the reading room at the Fox. That room is still called The Reading Room, but it is now the restaurant. In the long bar is a collection of beer mugs, and framed on the wall is an old newspaper of May 1891, exhorting the locals to 'Vote for Greene' as their Member of Parliament.

The food at the Fox is certainly not run of the mill. It is imaginative, tasty and plentiful. The lunchtime bar menu is wide-ranging. For instance, choose from farfalle pasta, trout, scallops in a crab and brandy sauce, spaghetti carbonara with bacon and wild mushrooms, chicken en croute and many more delights, all home-made. Two of the sweets available are iced Belgian chocolate marquise, or banana cream pie topped with a toffee fudge sauce. Half portions from the main menu can be ordered for children. The evening meals are mouth-watering, too. Greene King IPA, Abbot and XX Mild ales are sold. Taunton Dry cider is also served. Behind the pub is a paved area set with tables and chairs, facing south to the stream. Children will feel at home in the family room, and when not eating they can feed the ducks, or romp or play football in the pub's field, where there are mini goal nets. Well-behaved dogs are welcome.

The pub is open, and meals are served, at the usual hours but no food is available on Mondays. Booking is essential for Sunday lunch, while Sunday evening meals are served only by prior arrangement.

Telephone: 01359 230347.

How to get there: Pakenham is 5 miles east of Bury St Edmunds. Leave Bury on the A143 (towards Ixworth). In 4 miles turn right towards Thurston and almost immediately go left for Pakenham. From the east, leave the A14 at the Woolpit junction and travel on the A1088 towards Thetford. Go through Norton and in 1 mile turn left for Pakenham. The Fox is on the main village street.

Parking: The pub car park is quite large. The main street is wide enough to allow some parking.

Length of the walk: 3 miles (a short cut through Pakenham Wood is possible). Map: OS Landranger sheet 155 Bury St Edmunds and Sudbury area (inn GR 927672).

This is an easy walk, mostly on well-used footpaths and cart tracks. It starts along a broad green lane to the Thurston road. After a short length on the road, passing Pakenham Manor, the walk continues on a grass path leading along the edge of the recreation ground and then goes across marshy woodland, to cross a stream in the shallow valley bottom. The route is then on rising ground to the east of the village, circling Pakenham Wood. This is a delightful area, with a mixture of forest trees around a closely planted stand of conifers. From the northern edge of the wood are wide views of the valley of the Black Bourn. The return is across a sloping pasture beside Newe House, a fine old brick residence built in the early 17th century. The walk passes St Mary's church.

The Walk

Leave the Fox, going left up the main street until you are opposite a turning on the right called The Owell, a 'No Through Road'. On the corner on the

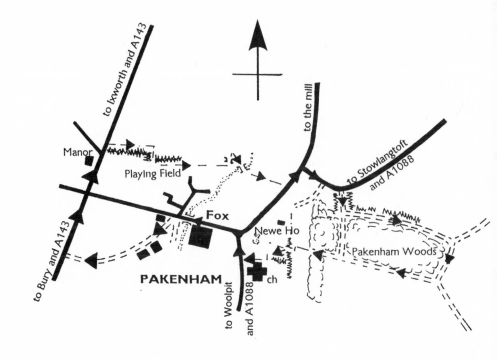

right is a deep and now wooded pit, belonging to the village, from which chalk was dug for grinding into whiting for ceilings and so on, long years ago. Do not go into The Owell but leave the road, going left, not on the track to Nether Hall, but on the adjacent track, signed 'Manor Farm'.

Follow this track, between hedges, for nearly ½ mile until you meet a road at right angles. Turn right and walk along the road up to the crossroads. Go straight over, passing Pakenham Manor and then a road off left. Go as far as the electricity wires that cross the road, and then turn right by the beech hedge and the footpath sign, onto a broad, grassy track. When the track goes right you too go right, and in 100 yards pass through a wide gap and turn left to walk beside the playing field, with the hedge on the left.

At the far end of the playing field, go through a gap in the cross-hedge and continue in the same direction, along a footpath which still has a hedge on the left, with well-tended gardens on the right. Follow this, past the rear of some garages, where you join a rough track.

When the track swings right, with the church in the distance, keep straight on along a grassy path, with the hedge on the left and woods on the right and dropping a little to go through a low-lying young plantation. Maybe you, too, may see a heron flying over. Presently, as you near a stream, you will see

Newe House, Pakenham.

an elegant wooden bridge, but first go left over a ditch on a two-sleeper footbridge, then go over the stream. Walk on through rustling poplars and out to the road.

Turn left towards the road junction where you take the right fork, towards Stowlangtoft and Badwell Ash. Climb the hill on the road, passing the entrance to Hamling House Hotel, hidden in the woods, and, shortly, pass a gravel cart track at the edge of the woods on the right. Keep along the road for a further 100 yards and then turn right up a green lane with hedges on both sides. When you come to Pakenham Wood, turn left along the well-used lane.

Should you want to make a short cut, you can continue straight on along a grassy track through the trees for 300 yards to rejoin the walk on the southern side of the wood.

For the main walk, keep beside Pakenham Wood on the right, on a track with a hedge on the left. When the hedge on the left ends, you will see stretching away, half-left, the valley of the Black Bourn, and beyond it the dwellings and farms comprising the parish of Stowlangtoft.

When you reach a three-way junction of tracks at the corner of the wood, follow the edge round to the right. In 250 yards there is another three-way junction. Here again swing right and continue to skirt the wood, passing under a large chestnut tree. Follow the broad, grassy headland path beside Pakenham Wood on the right. About 100 yards before the far corner of the field, pass on the right the woodland path which is the short cut mentioned earlier.

At the corner of the field go straight on through a narrow shelter belt of trees and cross a field to the far hedge. Go left for 10 yards, then right over the two-step stile into a pleasant field that slopes down to the village.

Go leftish down the field until you can see the church tower high on the left. Swing round left and climb towards a field corner, where a few steps lead up to a metal kissing-gate. Enter the churchyard and pass St Mary's, probably built not long after the Normans arrived, and out to the road.

Turn right, walk down the hill and then turn left into The Street to return to the Fox.

Places of interest nearby

At the edge of the village, about ¾ mile from The Street, are two mills about ½ mile apart. One, a *watermill*, beside the stream, and the other, a *windmill*, built in 1820, on the plateau. Both mills have been preserved, and both are capable of working.

Thorpe Morieux
The Bull Inn

This is a quiet, rural part of the county with gently undulating fields often cropped with cereals, sugar beet or oil-seed rape. Thorpe Morieux is a group of isolated farms and small hamlets. Nearby is the source of the river Brett which runs through Hadleigh, south to the river Stour. The church of St Mary the Virgin is in the centre of the village, near the road junction where the village sign proudly stands.

The Bull is a pleasant pub. The welcoming front is bright with flowers in summertime and the general atmosphere is relaxing. Some rather unusual features are the two tall wrought-iron poseur tables which were made in Croatia (in the midst of all their troubles).

The choice of food is interesting. You will find sirloin, T-bone or rump steak, hot 'n spicy chicken, broccoli and cream cheese pie, tagliatelle niçoise, chicken balinese and rice and four fillings for large Yorkshire puddings, among many other dishes. Then you could have treacle pudding, spotted dick, jam pudding or various gateaux and cheesecakes. Many different ales are stocked, though not all at the same time. They are selected from Burton Ale, Marston's Pedigree, Benskins, Tetley's, Directors, Royal Oak, Mauldons, Friary Meux, Burton Bridge, Spitfire and Adnams. Draught cider Cotton Head and Addlestones Best are kept. The pub is open, and

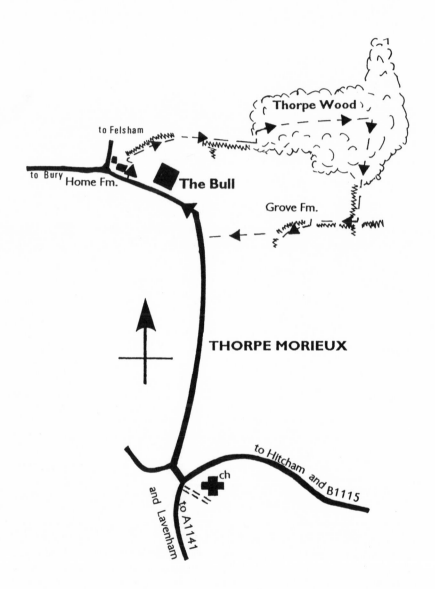

to Felsham

Thorpe Wood

to Bury

Home Fm.

The Bull

Grove Fm.

THORPE MORIEUX

to Hitcham and B1115

ch

and Lavenham

to A1141

meals are served, at the usual times except that on Saturdays it stays open until 4 pm. Children have their own menu, and they are made welcome. In the garden is a large climbing frame and a couple of swings. If well-behaved then dogs are welcome, too.
Telephone: 01284 828320.

How to get there: Thorpe Morieux is 5 miles north-east of Lavenham. From Lavenham follow the A1141, the Bury St Edmunds road, for 1½ miles. Turn right just before the water tower and follow the signs to Thorpe Morieux. At the three-way junction by the village sign, go north. The Bull is about a mile further on, towards Bradfield.

Parking: Behind the pub is a very large car park.

Length of the walk: 2 miles. Map: OS Landranger sheet 155 Bury St Edmunds and Sudbury area (inn GR 941548).

This short circular walk to Thorpe Wood uses grassy headland paths across pleasant, undulating arable farmland. It is a lonely and peaceful area.

The Walk

From the Bull go right. In 100 yards and just before Home Farm, the first building on the right, turn right on a wide, grassy path at the field edge. In just over 100 yards, turn left on a wide headland towards a barn. At the barn, go right on a headland, with a hedge on the left. Where the hedge ends keep along a grass path across the field with wide views to the left across a plateau. The path continues, with a hedge on the right, towards a wood. At the corner of the field go straight on through a gap in a hedge and immediately turn left on a grass lane between a hedge on the left and woods on the right. In 50 yards turn right along a narrow path into Thorpe Wood, which comprises a mixture of mature oaks and coppiced ash and hazel.

The path is waymarked. In 200 yards reach a sort of clearing where a grassy path joins from the left. Now go straight ahead and in 300 yards arrive at a place where there is a narrow forest ride to the left and right. It is not wide enough to be a firebreak and here, at a waymark, turn right, southward along a narrow footpath.

Eventually pass another waymark and then shortly afterwards leave the woods, at the corner of a large field.

Keep in the same direction on a grass headland path, with a hedge on the right, and when you get to the end of the field turn right at a waymark onto a wide, grass headland bridleway, with a hedge on the left. In just over 100 yards go left through the hedge at a waymark and continue, now with a hedge on the right. Where the hedge starts to swing round to the left, go

Village sign near the church at Thorpe Morieux.

right at a bridleway sign and continue on a headland, with a hedge on the right.

When the hedge ends, keep straight on along a rough margin between cultivation, under electricity wires. When you reach the road turn right and walk back to the Bull.

⑧ Hopton
The Vine

Hopton is a small village standing at a crossroads on slightly higher ground above the river Little Ouse, which, from its source in Redgrave Fen, 3 miles to the east, flows to join the Great Ouse river and thence to the sea at the Wash.

The Vine is believed to date from the 17th century. It is a pleasant country pub, with lots of nostalgia-inducing old farm implements around the walls. Above the bar there is a now outmoded Gunter's chain, as once used by surveyors. The whole of the frontage is taken up by public rooms, subtly subdivided. To the far left is a restaurant area.

Roast beef or pork, with roast potatoes, fresh vegetables and Yorkshire pudding is welcoming after a walk. Home-made steak pie, scampi, chicken nuggets, cod and lasagne are other items on the menu. If you are still hungry, you will find chocolate fudge or strawberry gateaux, banana split, apple pie and treacle tart to tempt you. Real ales such as Greene King IPA, Bass and Boddingtons are served. Dry Blackthorn cider is also available. Children are welcome and will enjoy the play apparatus in the garden. They may have half portions of anything from the menu. Dogs are not permitted on the premises.

The usual opening hours apply, but the inn is closed at Monday lunch-

times and food is not available on any evening. Sunday lunchtimes are very busy, so it might be a good idea to ring and book.
Telephone: 01953 681466.

How to get there: From Stanton, a village on the A143, Bury to Diss road, follow the B1111 for about 4 miles. The Vine is in the main street, on the left just beyond the church.

Parking: The pub car park is quite spacious.

Length of the walk: 3 miles. Map: OS Landranger sheet 144 Thetford, Breckland and surrounding area (inn GR 994792).

From the church, this easy walk starts along a well-used cart track over a small hill to the west of the village, where there are pleasant views. The walk then descends a little to skirt the Suffolk Wildlife Trust's Hopton Fen nature reserve, a remnant of the once extensive fens in the Waveney and Little Ouse valleys. It contains a wide variety of water loving plants and insects. The reeds and sedge are mown regularly. The return to the Vine is along a farm road and across field paths.

The Walk

Leave the Vine and go towards the church. A detour to look inside is worthwhile. The nave roof of 15th century All Saints is a very fine example of a hammer beam roof, the beams being carved figures, somewhat mutilated about the time of the Civil War by the Cromwellians, who detested graven images. See high in the east wall of the tower, inside the church, the sanctus bell window, from which the bell ringer watched the service, ready to ring the sanctus bell at the appropriate moment.

At the crossroads turn right down Nethergate Street past several lovely cottages, the chapel, the cemetery and, later, the flint-faced Old School House on the right. Turn right on a bridleway, a grassy cart track, which leads between the houses out to a field. Go straight on along the cart track, climbing slightly.

Enjoy the fine view of the Little Ouse valley, when you reach the summit of this small hill. At the next field boundary go left, descending slightly on a headland path, with a hedge on the right. At the corner of the field turn right. A sign shows that this is part of the Angles Way, a 77-mile long Regional Route from Great Yarmouth to Knettishall Heath.

In 20 yards go over a stile into Hopton Fen. Keep straight on along the edge of the fen and do not divert on a grass path to the left leading into the fen. The path swings to the right and becomes a headland path, with the fen on the left and Common Farm beyond the field on the right.

Keep to the waymarked path as it bears left and right round a corner of a

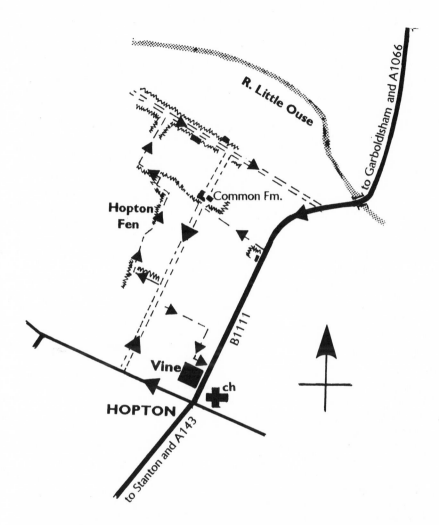

field. In the far corner, bear left over a footbridge and turn left, still along the Angles Way, across rough pasture, with the fen on the left. On reaching the corner of a field, your way is to the right, but first go straight on for a few yards, with gorse bushes on the right, and then circle to the right round the gorse bushes to reach a broad, grassy track interspersed with gorse bushes on both sides and with a wire fence on the right.

Go out through an iron gate into a lane, turn right and, leaving the Angles Way, walk along a broad track between hedges and fences. Pass on the right

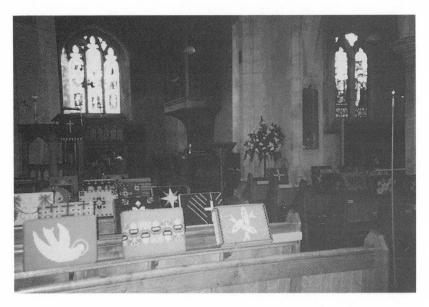

All Saints, Hopton.

a track to Common Farm, and keep straight on along a concrete farm road. On reaching the main road (the B1111), turn right. Pass a 30 mph sign and continue along the road, now swinging round to the left. Pass a pumping station and, just before a white house on the right, go right at a footpath sign along a cross-field path. Halfway across the field the path runs beside a hedge on the right, beyond which is white, thatched Common Farm.

Opposite the farmhouse, at a signpost, turn left onto a broad, grassy farm track. Half-left you can see the tower of the church. At the top of the slight hill pass the point where the path used earlier descends to the nature reserve.

In a little under 200 yards, at a sign, turn left on a well-used cross-field path. On the far side of the field turn right and walk beside a garden fence. Turn left and follow a narrow footpath between hedges out to the road and turn right to the Vine.

Places of interest nearby

Thelnetham Mill is open to the public now and again – on Sundays, July to September, at Easter and on bank holidays from 11 am to 7 pm, also most Saturdays during the year, and other times by arrangement. The mill is about 1½ miles east of Hopton. Telephone: 01359 250622. You can buy the mill's stoneground flour either at the mill, or at Chandlers at the crossroads in Hopton. *Knettishall Heath Country Park* is about 3 miles to the west.

Barking

9

The Barking Fox

Barking, a long village, extends about 2 miles from the church at the eastern end to Barking Tye, a large common in the west. On the southern side of the parish stand two large woods, good examples of woodlands which, years ago, provided a vital part of the rural economy in giving fuel and building materials. Priestley Wood, named after the scientist who discovered oxygen, is now owned by the Woodland Trust and Bonny Wood is a nature reserve.

The Barking Fox is a big, comfortable, popular pub which, besides catering for the lunchtime trade, has a large restaurant, resplendent in pink and white napery, with a carvery for the evening customers. Several changes of level add interest to the bars, linked by timber screens.

Some of the dishes to choose from are cod, fillet of plaice, chicken Kiev, chicken breast in a white wine and mushroom sauce, various steaks, and vegetarian dishes such as vegetable lasagne, tagliatelle niçoise and cracked wheat and walnut casserole. Just a few of the sweets on the menu are fresh fruit salad, peach melba, pear hélène, banana split, chocolate sin and raspberry meringue. Children are welcomed, and may eat either in the lounge or the restaurant. A range of food that appeals to them is offered, such as fish fingers and beefburger in a bun. A high chair is available. John Smith's real ale is served here, as is Strongbow draught cider. The Barking

Fox is open at the usual times. Dogs are not welcome in this pub. Telephone: 01449 722241.

How to get there: Barking is 3 miles south-west of Needham Market. From the A14, follow signs to Needham Market, then take the B1078 towards Wattisham and Ringshall. The Barking Fox is on the main road.

Parking: At the rear of the pub is a 100 space car park.

Length of the walk: 2½ miles. Map: OS Landranger sheet 155 Bury St Edmunds and Sudbury area (inn GR 067526).

The walk is along grassy headland paths and cart tracks. After a short section through a narrow belt of trees, the walk passes the entrance to Bonny Wood nature reserve. There are good views across rolling farmland to the north.

The Walk

Leave the Barking Fox and turn left along the wide verge beside the main road, passing a side road called Ladyfield. When opposite the middle pair of three similar pairs of cottages, leave the road, turning right by a footpath sign, up the field edge, with a black weatherboarded house behind a hedge on the left. Continue, with a ditch on your left. When that ditch goes left, carry straight on in the same direction as before, across the field towards the right end of a hedge, in the bottom of the shallow valley.

At the hedge-end go ahead for a couple of yards and then over a wooden footbridge with a handrail. Turn left and walk along the headland path, with a ditch on the left and the field rising to your right up towards the grid lines. Presently, at a crop division, a bank commences about 20 yards to your right. Go right, climb the yard-high bank, turn left, and again follow the headland path, with a ditch on the left. Half-right you can see Barking church. Soon a hedge begins at the bottom of the bank and you will pass alongside a paddock below. Just before a cream-washed house, a hedge goes down the bank to a stile. Go over the stile, swing right, passing the house on the left, and curve left between the house and its garage, to join a drive. Go right along a track, passing several cottages, and join the main road by Barking Forge, a working forge.

Go right along the road for 100 yards and, just after passing under the grid lines, turn right off the road at a footpath sign and climb up the hill on a headland path, with a hedge on the left.

Continue climbing, with both hedge and ditch on the left, under grid lines, and pass through a neck of the field where there is a tree-line and bank 100 yards away across the field. Pass under grid lines yet again and then you have Swingen's Wood now on your left. When this mixed wood

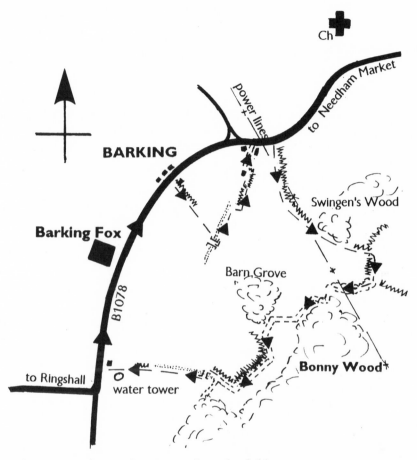

ends, carry on for another 100 yards to the field corner.

Close to the corner drop down to, and cross, a wooden footbridge. Turn right and follow the field edge until you come to a small wood on the right. Enter the wood, and walk on a narrow path which wanders through a curving, thin belt of trees.

After about 200 yards take an opportunity to go left across a shallow ditch, and leave the wood. Turn right and in 4 yards go under grid lines again and follow the field edge, with a ditch and a shelter belt on the right, for 100 yards.

At the field corner go straight ahead into the woods on an earth track, curving left then right to a junction of tracks. At this junction you will go right, but before doing so, walk left a bit to read the display board which tells about Bonny Wood. Return to the junction and walk out of the wood,

Barn Grove near Bonny Wood.

then go left on a track beside the trees. Where the wood boundary makes a bend to the left follow the track half-right for 150 yards across the field, to the edge of Barn Grove.

Swing left, and at the corner of Barn Grove cross a field to a high hedge. You can now see the green and white water tower which you will quite soon pass, away in Barking. Follow the track, alongside the hedge on the right. On the other side of this long, L-shaped field is Bonny Wood. Keep on the grassy cart track as it makes a sharp right turn, still following the hedge on the right.

At the field end, in the corner, where the track swings left across the field to the woods, you go very slightly right, down a little, on a well-worn path into the corner of another field, with a ditch on your left. Cross the three-sleeper footbridge with no handrail, turn right and walk along the field edge to the water tower.

Passing the tower on your left, keep on alongside a meadow and in the next corner bear right to join a lane, going past a cottage and out to the road by a filling station and the post office. Turn right and walk alongside the Tye, back to the Barking Fox.

⑩ Wortham
The Dolphin Inn

Wortham lies about 3 miles from South Lopham Fen, the source of the Waveney, the infant river forming the northern boundary of this parish of isolated settlements. The main centre is the buildings, including the Dolphin, which are ranged around Long Green, the largest unenclosed village green remaining in Suffolk. This is a tract of natural grassland, dotted here and there with isolated trees and shrubs, upon which local people would have had common rights to graze livestock. You may still see animals grazing here. There are a number of similar greens in this part of Suffolk, including Great Green which is visited in the walk. Wortham is featured in *The Biography of a Victorian Village*, written and illustrated by Richard Cobbold, who was the rector here for 52 years in the 19th century. He also wrote several other books, including *Margaret Catchpole* and *Freston Tower* both based on local happenings or places.

The 16th century Dolphin is a large, but not impersonal, pub with a warm welcome. At one time the parish boundary between Wortham and Burgate actually ran through the pub. 'Beating the Bounds' is a ceremony usually held in May, on Rogation Sunday, when the boundary is walked, and at various points on the route a small child used to be turned upside down and his head gently bumped on the ground – the idea being to imprint on his memory the position of the boundary. Of course, in Wortham the people formerly had to go in the front door of the Dolphin, through the pub and out of the back door. There is also a story about a 13-year old boy who was living at the inn in 1830. He was a pauper but received no Parish Relief because his bedroom was astride the boundary – 5 inches of his bed was in Wortham and the rest in Burgate. Since he did not reside wholly in either parish both denied him help!

The home-cooked fare at the Dolphin is delicious. On the long menu are rump, sirloin, fillet and T-bone steaks, lamb balti with rice and naan bread, beef stroganoff, Surf and Turf, pheasant forestière, roast Norfolk duck in a Caesar sauce, chicken Penang, Thai-style chicken with noodles and dreamy kleftico – lamb with fresh vegetables. Home-made desserts include sticky toffee pudding, spotted dick, orange and chocolate torte, treacle sponge pudding and blackberry and apple pie. The real ales served are Adnams Bitter, John Smith's, Marston's Pedigree and, in winter, Adnams Old. Red Rock draught cider is on sale, too. Children are welcomed. They have their own menu, and they may eat in the restaurant. There is space for play outdoors and the aviary with its many brightly coloured finches will interest them. The Dolphin has the usual opening hours, and meals are served at all times. Dogs, if well-behaved, are also welcome.

Telephone: 01379 898401.

How to get there: Wortham is 3 miles south-west of Diss, on the A143 Diss to Bury St Edmunds road. The Dolphin is beside the main road through the village. At the time of writing, a new road, which ends close to the edge of Wortham, is under construction, so follow the signs.

Parking: At the rear of the pub is an ample car park. There is also plenty of room on the old road which runs in front of the pub.

Length of the walk: 3½ miles. Map: OS Landranger sheet 144 Thetford, Breckland and surrounding area (inn GR 082771).

This is an easy walk, most of which uses minor roads and cart tracks. The route starts along Wortham Long Green, then takes a footpath and a minor road to Great Green, which lies in the neighbouring parish of Burgate. After skirting this green and approaching St Mary's church, the return is on a well-used cart track, Bean's Lane, back to Wortham.

The Walk

From the Dolphin go right, passing the isolated three arches, with their inscription, 'Faith', 'Hope' and 'Charity', which are all that remains of the former reading room. Cross the main road to the junction with the road to Roydon. Do not go along that road but go sharp left across the green to pick

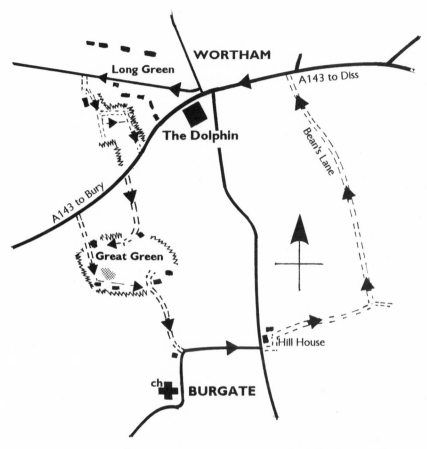

up the road through the middle of Long Green, which leads to Redgrave.
Dotted around the green are a number of farms and cottages.

Keep alongside the road and pass a white house on the left. Shortly after,
at a footpath marker and a sign saying 'Deo Gratias', turn left along a
concrete drive towards a farm. Just before the farmhouse turn half-left onto
a cart track which leads through an iron gate.

Pass an open-fronted barn on the right and make your way through the
nursery garden. The official right of way is straight on for 200 yards, left to
the boundary of the field and then right along the headland. If the way is not
clearly visible on the ground, follow cart tracks leading in a similar direction.

At the road, the A143, turn right for 100 yards and then go left down the
tarmac road to Great Green. The road bends to the right by the Methodist
chapel, where it becomes a gravel drive. In 200 yards you come to the edge

Cottage at Great Green.

of the green, where the road you are on divides into several cart tracks leading to various properties. Here, turn right on a grassy cart track which skirts the green.

In 100 yards, pass on the right a white, thatched cottage and, a few yards further on, turn left on a gravel drive which leads to the southern side of the green. Reach a small pond on the left and swing left on a grassy track along the southern edge, passing Claybanks, a cream-painted house.

Facing Great Green on the perimeter are several farm houses and cottages and the boundary hedge contains many mature trees. Continue along the edge of the green, passing a pair of brick cottages, West End Cottage and East Cottage.

At the south-east corner pass, on the left, an old lift pump, fixed above a well which once provided the water for the nearby dwellings. Turn right when you reach a narrow tarmac lane and climb a slight rise. Straight ahead is Burgate church. The lane bends left and comes to a three-way road junction with a large oak tree in the centre of a grass triangle.

Turn left on the road to Mellis. In about ¼ mile, at a T-junction, go straight over through a farmyard, passing a barn surmounted by an elaborate weather vane on the right. Bear left a little, and then right, with Hill Farm house on the left.

Go along the well-used gravelly cart track for about ¼ mile. Ignoring minor tracks straight ahead, turn sharp left and continue along the main track. You will soon come to a hedge on the left and you are on a broad, grassy path. Go through a wide cross-hedge and keep straight on along a cart track. Now there is a fence on the right. The track leads into a leafy lane for about 100 yards, then continues straight across a field, with a fence to the right, and out to the road, the A143.

Turn left and use the footway on the north side of the road for about ¼ mile to return to the Dolphin.

⑪ Brantham
The Bull

Brantham is a large village on high land overlooking the head of the Stour estuary, a 10-mile long tidal inlet extending from Felixstowe to Manningtree. On the opposite shore, is the Essex village of Mistley. At times you can see cargo ships berthed on the waterfront there. This wide stretch of calm water is, however, generally a quiet area with fewer craft than on the Orwell and the Deben rivers. Upstream of Manningtree, to the west, the river Stour flows through the Dedham Vale, which has been famously portrayed in several paintings by the artist, John Constable.

The Bull has two bars, the large, L-shaped one to the left of the main door, devoted mainly to eating, with beams and a grey-blue and pink decor, and a smaller one where there are bar games. The walls are enlivened by posters, sketches and photos of shows from the landlord's long stage career. From the extensive gardens there are fine views of the Stour.

On the menu are fresh cod or haddock fillet, chilli con carne, gammon steak with pineapple and chips, fisherman's platter, American burger or cheeseburger, home-made steak and kidney pie, lasagne and garlic chicken and chips, plus a variety of vegetarian dishes. To follow, you can choose from spotted dick, rhubarb crumble, jam sponge and many other delights, all with cream. Coffee comes with a jug of cream, rather than those impossibly difficult to open mini UHT cartons. Real ales such as Greene King IPA and a guest beer are on sale, as well as Red Rock draught cider. Children are welcome here and they may have half portions from the menu. In the garden there are large aviaries, pet rabbits and a raised pond with goldfish (supervision near the pond is wisely insisted upon). The Bull is open at lunchtimes and in the evenings seven days a week for meals and for drinking. Dogs are not allowed in the pub.

Telephone: 01473 328494.

How to get there: The Bull at Brantham is on the A137, Ipswich to Manningtree road, at its junction with the B1080 to Holbrook.

Parking: The pub car park is large. On the opposite side of the road is a council layby which can accommodate several cars.

Length of the walk: 2½ miles (a short cut saving ½ mile is possible). Map: OS Landranger sheet 169 Ipswich and The Naze area (inn GR 122345).

From the walk you will get wide views over the Stour estuary to the Essex shoreline. You may well see ducks and wading birds and possibly a heron or two.

The Walk
Leave the Bull and turn left along the A137 towards Manningtree. In 100 yards, just after the last house on the left, turn left down a tarmac lane, with a hedge on the right and, at first, a hedge on the left, too.

Pass Seafield House with its crinkle-crankle garden wall, which curves in and out in a series of arcs to give additional strength to the structure. Where a track goes off right towards Brantham Hall Farm keep straight ahead, still on a hard farm road with grass in the middle. Stretching ahead you can see the Stour estuary and beyond it the shoreline of Essex. Soon leave the farm track and continue on a grassy headland path, with a hedge on the right, straight towards the river. Turn right along the flood protection bank, which we call the river wall.

In ¼ mile, where the river wall makes a sudden snake to the left, and then right, drop down off the wall to the end of Hall Lane, a private track leading inland to Brantham Hall. Continue straight ahead through a gap beside a footpath sign along a grassy path, which at first is parallel to the river wall about 30 yards away on the left, but the path and the river wall gradually diverge.

Do not go left towards a long row of mature willow trees, but keep roughly straight on, parallel to the willows and 40–50 yards away. This is a wide, grass path through rough ground with reeds, beside a plantation of young, slender willows.

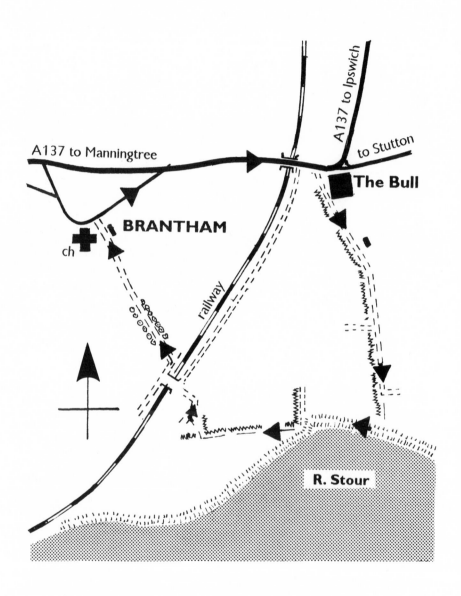

The river Stour at Brantham.

About 100 yards from the end of the willow plantation, go right over a stile (or through the adjacent gap) up a few steps into another field, in the corner of which is a small stand of oak trees. Just beyond the trees you join a farm track coming in from the left. Bear right along the track but pause for a moment to look at the wide view of Manningtree and the head of the estuary.

The farm track rises. Do not go left to a concrete storage area, but keep on the gravel path, which soon leads to a bridlebridge over the railway.

For a short cut back to the Bull, take the cart track to the right and follow the railway fence to the A137.

For the main walk, go straight ahead over the bridge and, immediately after, turn right for about 30 yards and then turn left along a narrow, tree-lined tarmac road. At the end of the avenue you can see Brantham church ahead, behind some trees. Go straight on to reach the churchyard. Turn left at the gate and cross the churchyard to leave by the rather fine lychgate which has carvings on the under side of its wood-shingled roof. On the west side of the tower are a pair of gargoyles and, on the tower, golden St Michael, carrying a cross, points into the wind.

Turn right on leaving the lychgate, and walk along the quiet country road to join the A137. Cross the road and go right, along the footway and over the railway bridge. Fast traffic uses this road, so take great care when you cross over it to the Bull.

Hoxne
The Swan

At the northern edge of Suffolk, in the valley of the river Waveney, stands the village of Hoxne (pronounced to rhyme with oxen). Its buildings cluster round a small yet delightful village green at the foot of rising ground, upon which stands the church. However, like many Suffolk villages, Hoxne parish includes several other separate groups of dwellings some distance from the centre. Tradition and legend say that St Edmund, the Saxon King of East Anglia, was martyred at Hoxne. There is a stone obelisk, in fields a bit south of the village green, which is said to mark the site of his death, where Danish invaders tied him to a tree and shot him through with arrows. Whilst the story of St Edmund is somewhat speculative, there is no doubt that Hoxne has a history. In recent times a farm worker dug up a large hoard of Roman coins and other treasure. The treasure is now with the British Museum.

The Swan is a very old pub. It was built about 1480 by the Bishop of Norwich, and the atmosphere is olde worlde. The walls are timber-framed, beams abound, the enormous fireplace, at least 10 ft wide, is deep and a big wood fire burns therein in winter. There are a pair of fire dogs for carrying a spit roast and a swinging arm from which hangs a gleaming copper kettle. Wicker baskets of all shapes and sizes, full of dried flowers, are around the room. The Swan has a cosy restaurant and three other welcoming public rooms. Outside is a very large, sunken lawn, around which are tables and benches, a fine prospect for summer evenings. Trees surround the whole.

An extensive menu includes Indian-style grilled chicken strips, spaghetti with prawn, tomato and garlic sauce, lamb kidneys, sausage and lentil hotpot, pancakes filled with mushrooms and cheese, smoked salmon, crab mousse, lamb cutlets and hash browns with bacon and eggs. To follow, choose from lemon cheesecake, chocolate pots, bread and butter pudding, Jamaican bananas (baked in rum) and sticky toffee pudding. Children are welcome, if sitting quietly at a table with their parents.

In early November an exultant notice appears in the porch, 'Adnams Old Ale is back' – this ale is only brewed in the winter. Other real ales served are Adnams Bitter, Greene King Abbot and, again in winter only, Tally Ho. The pub is open from noon to 2.30 pm and from 5.30 pm to 11 pm on weekdays, and stays open to 3.30 pm on Saturday afternoons. Standard Sunday hours apply. Meals are served at the usual times, except Sunday evenings when no food is available. It is necessary to book to eat in the restaurant on Saturday evenings and at Sunday lunchtimes. Well-behaved dogs are allowed.

Telephone: 01379 668275.

How to get there: Hoxne lies on the B1118 Diss to Stradbroke road, about 6 miles from Stradbroke. From the east and west take the A143 road between Bury St Edmunds and Lowestoft and join the A140 road, from Ipswich and the south, at Scole. The B1118, signed 'Stradbroke', 'Oakley' and 'Hoxne', joins the A140 just south of the Scole bypass. In 2½ miles, where the B1118 turns sharp left, keep straight on to reach the Hoxne village green and the Swan in 300 yards.

Parking: Beside the pub is a large car park. A few yards further north there are several spaces alongside the green.

Length of the walk: 2½ miles. Map: OS Landranger sheet 156 Saxmundham, Aldeburgh and surrounding area (inn GR 180772).

From the village green the walk goes past the church and along the pretty Watermill Lane, down close to the river Waveney, passing near the watermill. The return is along quiet lanes and over footpaths back to the village.

The Walk

Turn northwards from the Swan and keep to the right of the village green, a triangle of grass upon which stands a seat covered with a tiled roof. At the far corner of the green continue straight up a narrow lane towards the church. At the top, after the lane becomes narrower, reach a road, the B1118, and turn right.

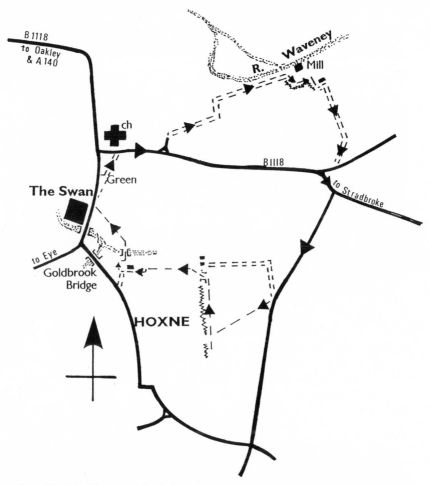

Pass Church Close on the left and in 100 yards turn left down Watermill Lane. Keep on the tarmac lane as it makes a sharp turn to the right. After further bends to left and then right, you are walking beside a meadow sloping down to the left. On the far side of the field is the mill stream and beyond it, a further field away, the river Waveney.

At the point where the lane swings slightly left and descends towards a white house, and beyond it the weatherboarded three-storey mill building, go right at a signpost along a concrete farm road leading through a metal gate, to swing left passing a row of farm sheds.

The concrete ends at the last shed but keep straight on along a grass path. Cross a stile beside a gate and turn right, then follow a grassy lane as it

Goldbrook Bridge beneath which King Edmund hid.

curves to the left between a hedge and a row of trees. Soon after passing a cottage on the left, turn right on a gravel farm road. In the distance you can see, over to the right, the tower of Hoxne church. The track passes a white house on the left and then becomes a surfaced road with hedges on both sides. Very soon come to a T-junction opposite Gate House Farm and turn right.

In 100 yards reach the B1118 and turn left towards Stradbroke. Please take extreme care here because the main road makes a right and left bend and there is insufficient provision for pedestrians. After about 100 yards, leave the main road, turning right on the road towards Hoxne Cross Street.

Follow this minor road down into a shallow valley, to cross a tiny stream and continue up the other side. Pass a concrete hardstanding on the right. A little further on, where the road swings slightly left, a hedge on the right starts and a concrete drive goes off to the right to the Anglian Water Treatment Works. From here take the signed cross-field footpath on a line roughly towards the left-hand side of a group of silos, which you can see two fields away.

Should the path be obstructed, or difficult to use, the concrete drive will take you in the right direction – see sketch map.

Reach, at the far side of the field, a narrow, grassy headland path. Turn right along it, with a hedge and a ditch on the left. Soon you will come to high chain link fencing which indicates the corner of the Water Treatment

Works. Turn left over a sleeper bridge and then continue on a narrow footpath between the substantial fence on the right and a light fence on the left. After leaving the works on the right, pass a young plantation of mixed woodland.

The fence on the left makes a short dog-leg left and right. At this point the official right of way turns half-right, but we suggest following the land-owner's proposed diversion, as on the sketch map. Keep beside the fence on the left and pass a house on the right. Just beyond the house turn right and follow the waymarked route round the outbuildings, to a long foot-bridge.

Cross the bridge and continue along a narrow footpath, eventually coming to a broad, grass path, with a trimmed hedge on the right and a paddock on the left. This path becomes a lane serving a row of houses on the right and soon joins the village street opposite the Swan.

⑬ Brandeston
The Queen's Head

Brandeston is a small village, with picturesque cottages fronting both sides of the street. The river Deben meanders through on its way from Debenham to the head of its tidal estuary at Melton. During the Civil War the bigoted, evil witch-finder Matthew Hopkins allegedly 'found' an octogenarian vicar of Brandeston to be a witch, at a so-called court held in the inn, and the poor old man was hanged in Bury St Edmunds. This is depicted in the village sign.

This attractive old pub, the Queen's Head, is set well back from the road in spacious grounds. It has three quite separate areas. One is a family eating room, quiet and comfortable, set with tables and Windsor chairs, another bar is on the other side of the entrance hall, and the third you would probably not find at all, were it not signed from the frontage, as it has its own entrance at the rear of the pub. On the walls there are photographs and interesting old documents. The pub offers bed and breakfast, and there is a caravan and camping site attached.

The range of dishes offered includes home-baked gammon, home-made lasagne, chicken goujons, chilli with rice, nut and mushroom pancakes and spicy pork. Sweets to choose from are Queen's pudding, gateau pear belle helène, caramel choux, steamed blackberry and apple sponge pudding, chocolate roulade and apricot crumble. For Friday and Saturday evenings there is a special menu. Children dining with their parents are welcome. They can have half portions from the main menu, as well as such old favourites as beefburgers, sausages and baked beans. The large garden, dotted with lime trees, has in it a climbing 'tree', a slide and a swing, and of course space to run around in.

Such real ales as Adnams Bitter, Broadside and Mild are on sale here, as is Strongbow draught cider. The pub is open at the usual times. Meals are served at lunch and in the evening, with the exception of Sunday evenings. Obedient dogs are welcome.

Telephone: 01728 685307.

How to get there: Brandeston lies about 3 miles south-west of Framlingham. Use the A1120, which is the cross-country road between Stowmarket and Yoxford, to go to Earl Soham, where you turn south to Brandeston about 2 miles away. The Queen's Head is on the left, set well back from the road.

Parking: You will find a large car park at the Queen's Head. There is little other parking in the village, except on an occasional roadside verge.

Length of the walk: 2 miles or 3 miles. Map: OS Landranger sheet 156 Saxmundham, Aldeburgh and surrounding area (inn GR 249606).

This is a pleasant, leisurely walk through part of the upper reaches of the Deben valley. Passing close to the church and Brandeston Hall, now a school, it takes a lane down to cross the river Deben. After skirting several fields and woods the way recrosses the Deben and goes alongside the school playing field. From here it is possible, for a shorter walk, to return directly to the start. The full 3-mile walk continues along a road back to the river, to follow a riverside meadow for a short distance before climbing away from the river, and returning through the attractively rural village street.

The Walk

From the Queen's Head go out to the road and cross straight over to walk along the road which leads towards Brandeston Hall. At the T-junction turn left.

However, you may wish to divert a short way to look at All Saints' church, which can be seen half-right, and from the far side of the churchyard you can see something of Brandeston Hall. The Hall is an interesting building which, having only been built in 1864, is not nearly as old as it looks. It is the junior department of Framlingham College.

Having turned left, keep on along the road for about 200 yards. When you reach a road junction, with a large grass triangle on the left, turn right and go down a green lane. Where a track swings sharply left, keep slightly right and

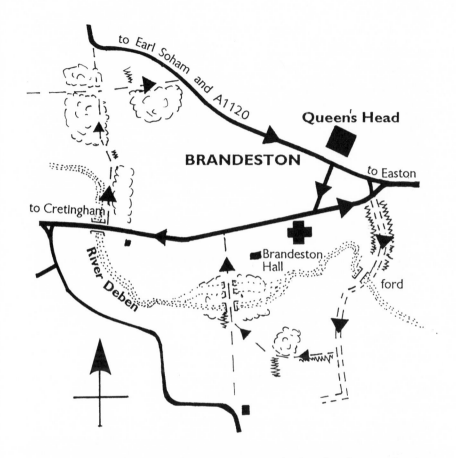

go down towards the river, where there is a ford with a long pedestrian bridge beside it. Continue along the track through a small willow plantation and then turn left at a sign, along a wide headland path beside a hedge. Glance behind you for a view of Brandeston Hall.

On reaching the end of the field, and 20 to 30 yards from an isolated farmhouse, turn right at a sign along a headland path, with a hedge on the left. At the next corner go slightly left through a hedge and continue beside the wood on the right. Looking back, the tower of Hoo church can be seen in the distance. Hoo is a reference to a slight hill.

In the corner of the field go over a stile without a footpiece, into a pasture, and head towards an electricity pole. Walk down the hill towards a hedge in the valley bottom near the corner where the hedge meets a wood. Cross another stile without a footpiece, into a narrow path between hedges.

Brandeston Hall.

The path crosses a bridge over the river Deben and continues through a small wood and over two further bridges. Beyond the wood follow a grassy path alongside a row of mature trees out to a road.

For the shorter walk, turn right here. Just beyond the church turn left to return to the Queen's Head.

For the main walk, turn left along the road and you will eventually, in just over ¼ mile, come to where the road drops steeply down towards Brandeston Bridge over the Deben.

Just before the bridge, and at the start of the steel guard railings, go right at the footpath sign on a narrow path through a young plantation of willows. In about 200 yards cross a stile into a meadow beside the river. Follow alongside the woods on the right. Where the woods end, bear half-left beside a hedge on the right (note: do not go straight on through the hedge on a well-worn cattle track). After passing a few isolated trees on the left, and ignoring a long gap in the hedge on the right, reach the corner of the meadow. Cross a stile, followed by a sleeper bridge, into mixed woodland.

Keep on the narrow footpath parallel to the edge of the woods and go across a small clearing and then through a short blackthorn tunnel to reach, at right angles, a grassy woodland path. Turn right.

Leave the wood and go over a dilapidated stile to follow a wide, grassy headland path up the hill. In 200 yards pass woods on the right. Go over a gate into a pasture and continue beside the woods. At the corner of the field, cross a stile and turn right along the road to return to the Queen's Head, ½ mile away.

Places of interest nearby

Easton Farm Park is a working farm plus a lot more. You can watch cows being milked and see several breeds of pigs, and lots of birds. Children can feed some of the smaller animals. There are various demonstrations – and a working blacksmith. A large, well-equipped play area enables children to let off steam. Opening times are 10.30 am to 6 pm daily from mid-March to October. Telephone: 01728 746475.

⑭ Framlingham
The White Horse

Near the source of the river Ore, which flows out to the Alde estuary, and on a plateau of arable farmland, lies the small and compact town of Framlingham with its fascinating castle. The triangular-shaped Market Hill is surrounded by tightly packed dwellings and shops and just above it, on a slight hill, is St Michael's church. On the north side the land drops steeply to the Mere, which is a lake surrounded by marshes, now a nature reserve. It is said that the Mere was formed when the castle was built.

The White Horse inn is quite large, but is subdivided into small, intimate areas. Situated by Well Close Square, it is near the hub of Framlingham life and yet quiet. It was built as three cottages about 1600, but by 1680 they had been converted into a pub. There are many exposed timber beams. In the summer everywhere is bright with hanging flower baskets.

The food is plentiful and well served. On the menu are roast chicken, gammon steak with wedge potatoes and salad, White Horse Whopper, chicken nuggets, breaded plaice, sausage, egg and chips, and cheese omelette. A wide, and changing, range of home-made sweets include banana long boat, Heaven on Earth – a chocolate creation – peanut pie, apple pie, meringue mountain, and grasshopper pie (mint and chocolate). Real ales on offer are Webster's and John Smith's.

The inn is open at the usual times, but in winter no meals are served on Sunday evenings. The olde worlde non-smoking restaurant is open for evening meals, except on Sundays and Mondays. Children are welcomed. There is a dining area for them away from the bar, and high chairs are available. The garden is large, with plenty of room to kick a ball about. Dogs are not allowed in the pub, but they may go in the garden if on a lead.

Telephone: 01728 723220.

How to get there: From the south, use the A12 Ipswich to Lowestoft road, then the B1116 from the grade-separated junction just east of Wickham Market, to reach Framlingham in 5 miles. Alternatively, use the A1120 Stowmarket to Yoxford road and turn off at Saxtead Green on the B1119 or at Badingham on the B1120.

Parking: There is a good car park at the White Horse. In addition there is a public car park just to the north of Well Close Square.

Length of the walk: 2½ miles (or, being a figure-of-eight, it can easily be divided into two shorter walks). Map: OS Landranger sheet 156 Saxmundham, Aldeburgh and surrounding area (inn GR 282634).

This pleasant walk takes you through the most historic parts of Framlingham town, then across open country to the east and back past the castle and the Mere.

The Walk

From the White Horse inn go across the square into Bridge Street and continue on round. When you reach triangular Market Hill go left up Church Lane and climb the steps into St Michael's churchyard. The church is a fine, large, 15th century edifice built in the perpendicular style. It contains many memorials and tombs of the Howard family, former owners of the castle.

Swing round to the right to pass the south porch, and go on past the priest's door, half-hidden behind a flying buttress, and out to meet Church Street. Cross straight over into Double Street, with its interesting houses. At the far end, at the junction with Castle Street, see the Victorian octagonal letter box, one of only three in East Anglia – one other is also in Framlingham and the third is outside King's College, Cambridge.

You will return to this point later on the route. *For any who want a shorter walk,* turn left here and proceed to the castle.

For the main walk, turn right along Castle Street and at the crossroads go right into Fore Street. After 100 yards swing left off the road onto a public footpath, a green lane with hedges both sides and some mature trees.

The track, now in an open field, turns a field corner to the left and presently the main track swings right. At that point go straight ahead, with a

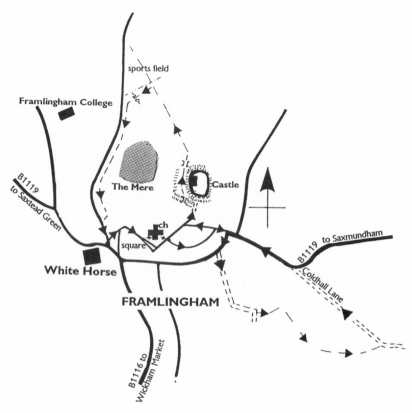

ditch on the left and a hedge on the right, climbing as you go. Pass a cartbridge on the left, and at the end of the field bear round to the right. At a T-junction of broad green paths go left. Carry on out to the road, where a sign points back the way you came, 'Public Bridleway North Green'. Turn left along the road and walk towards Framlingham.

At the crossroads where you were earlier, cross straight over into Castle Street, passing the end of Double Street and go on to the end, where you turn right towards the castle.

The castle as it is today dates from about 1200, but both a fort and a stone castle were there before that. The curtain wall is about 40 ft high, with 13 towers.

Just before reaching the gatehouse go left through a turnstile and down the path. Go right over a wooden footbridge, and immediately left, up to the edge of the castle grounds and go right. Walk along with views over the Mere and Framlingham College beyond. At the end drop down, go over a wooden footbridge, then a stile and go straight on. Pass through a gate and take the left fork, walking with mature trees on the right.

Framlingham Castle from the castle walls.

A few yards before the path enters the Framlingham College sports field, go left through a wooden pedestrian gate and walk on a permissive path along the perimeter of a meadow. In about 100 yards go over a footbridge and rejoin the definitive path.

Pass through a series of meadows around the Mere, managed by the Suffolk Wildlife Trust. All the meadows have names, and information boards describe the habitats. For instance, Hither Long Meadow, close by the Mere, is a popular feeding-spot for migrating birds, especially waders.

Keep going on until a wooden kissing-gate leads you up into a car park. Go right, out to the road, opposite Sir Robert Hitcham's Almshouses of 1654, and go left along New Road back to Well Close Square once more, and the White Horse.

Places of interest nearby
A walkway at the top of the curtain wall allows visitors to walk all the way round *Framlingham Castle.* Down below, within the walls, the 18th century Poor House is intact. It houses a museum of local artefacts, including an acetylene cycle lamp (pre-World War II). The castle is open from 10 am to 6 pm during April to October, and from 10 am to 4 pm in the winter months, November to March. Telephone: 01728 724189.

⑮ Waldringfield
The Maybush

Waldringfield is a boating centre on the west shore of the Deben estuary. In summer the river is a popular sailing area, and small craft of all kinds pass to and fro along the water. In winter there are far fewer boats and the estuary becomes a wild and lonely place, inhabited by ducks, geese and wading birds.

The Maybush is a favourite haunt of yachtsmen. Everywhere you look in the pub you see pictures, model ships, brass fittings and many things appertaining to boats. In one corner is a large model of the *Cutty Sark*. A free-standing fire warms the areas on both sides of it on cold days. The pub lies at the end of a winding road through this pretty village, where low cliffs stand above the river shore. The pub was first licensed in 1745, and was then called the Cliff Inn.

On the menu are fillet of plaice or haddock, chicken curry, rice and poppadums, chilli, steak and kidney pudding, steak and Guinness pie and an array of cold meats or pork pie with chips and pickles, or salad. Sweets include apple strudel and ice-creams. The real ales served are Flowers Original, Greene King IPA, Bass and Tolly Cobbold. Dry Blackthorn draught cider is on sale. The pub is open, and meals are available, seven days a week both at lunchtime and in the evenings. There is a family room and a special

children's menu. The garden above the cliffs has plenty of play apparatus, and the beach is very close. Dogs are not welcome in the pub.
Telephone: 01473 736215.

How to get there: Waldringfield is 7 miles east of Ipswich. From the A14, at the grade-separated junction on the south-east side of Ipswich, take the A12, going north. In 2 miles, at a roundabout, take the minor road to Waldringfield. Continue until the road ends at the river bank, by the Maybush.

Parking: The pub has its own large car park, and there is also a public car park alongside it, on the cliff top.

Length of the walk: 2 miles or 3 miles. Map: OS Landranger sheet 169 Ipswich and The Naze area (inn GR 285445).

This walk starts and finishes alongside the river Deben and at other points on the route you will see wide views of the estuary. By the salt marshes at the northern end of the walk there is a particularly fine view of the river with distant views of Woodbridge, its church and its windmill. Low tide reveals wide stretches of mud upon which many species of wildfowl dabble and poke around for food. Small boats sailing on the calm waters or moored beside the shore are a delight to watch.

The Walk
From the Maybush make your way down to the riverside and turn right along the shore. The innovative anti-litter painting, and its message, may long be remembered by children, and possibly adults too.

After about 100 yards leave the shore and climb a gravel drive onto the river bank, passing the Waldringfield Sailing Club building. Soon, at a dinghy park, go right for about 10 yards and then left, in front of a row of small chalets on your right.

At the end of the huts, with salt marshes ahead, turn sharp right at the footpath sign and walk towards what looks like a small garage, then keep on the path, swinging left and right, past the garage. Shortly, where a track goes right, keep straight on along a narrower footpath and soon skirt a small lake on the left. When you reach a minor cart track at the head of the lake, turn left. Pass between two lakes and go straight ahead, climbing slightly, to a gap in a mature hedge. There is a footpath sign here.

Follow a sandy cart track across an arable field. As you rise you get an extensive view of the river on the left. Pass through a gap in a sparse hedge, and keep straight on along a well-used path across another arable field.

Go to a gap in a hedge just left of a house, White Hall. Follow the garden wall on the right and when you get to the end of the garden on the right, turn right on a grassy lane which soon joins a track from the house.

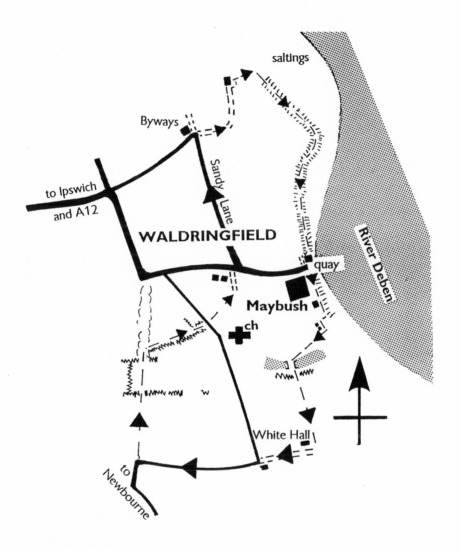

Continue straight on along a well-used track with grass in the middle, soon to pass a cottage on the left and come out to a road at a bend. Keep straight on.

When this quiet road makes a sharp turn to the left, turn right at a footpath sign and walk across an arable field. Some 2½ miles away on the left, is the large concrete tower of the British Telecom Research Station. Go through a field boundary in the shade of a large oak tree. Continue straight

The river Deben at Waldringfield.

on parallel to the hedge on the left. On the far side of this field go straight ahead through a narrow gap in the hedge (footpath sign) which leads into a path through a narrow wood of mixed vegetation.

In 100 yards, by a footpath sign at a T-junction, go right along a well-used broad headland path beside a hedge on the right. At the end of the field continue on a narrow footpath, which leads into a narrow path with thick, trimmed hedges on both sides. Cross straight over a road. On the right you may see the brick tower of Waldringfield church. Keep on a well-used path across an arable field, making roughly for a point 50 yards to the right of a black-painted, timber-faced house. On the far side of the field turn left along a short lane, and reach the village street. Turn right.

For the shorter walk, the Maybush is 300 yards further along the road.

For the main walk, go 25 yards towards the river and turn left down Sandy Lane. Pass the Old Post Office on the right, and later pass an Anglian Water pumping station on the right.

In about ¼ mile from the village street, Sandy Lane makes a sharp left turn by a white-roofed house called Byways. At this point turn right on a broad cart track with grass in the middle. In 100 yards the hedge on the right ends, and the cart track swings gradually round to the left. After 200 yards the track swings to the right in front of a white bungalow. Pass on the left a brick two-storey building with garage doors and then continue between

73

lush vegetation, on a narrow footpath which makes several twists and turns but eventually comes out on the riverside salt marsh.

Here swing right on a grassy path on the edge of the salt marsh. Very soon climb onto the river flood protection wall and keep on it for nearly ½ mile. You may notice that the marsh on the left, which is occasionally covered by the sea on high spring tides, is much higher than the fields on the right, which are protected by the river wall.

The path on the wall leads back to Waldringfield. Turn inland at the boatyard for about 50 yards to a narrow road and then go left to the Maybush.

⑯ Rumburgh
The Rumburgh Buck

South of Bungay, on a plateau of rich arable land, lies a group of villages, collectively known as the Saints. These parishes each bear a saint as a suffix or prefix to their name. For example, there are St James South Elmham, All Saints South Elmham, Ilketshall St Margaret and Ilketshall St James, to name but four. Rumburgh is on the southern edge of this area and once was the site of an abbey,

The Rumburgh Buck is a delightful, cosy, olde worlde pub with lots of small, intimate dining and drinking areas. All tastes are catered for. There are quiet areas where just a few little groups of friends gather round a roaring fire, a spacious room for bar games at the far end of the pub, away from the rest, and a restaurant for somewhat larger gatherings, or for parties perhaps, with settles to give a friendly atmosphere. Deep in one large fireplace an array of copper utensils sparkle in wintertime firelight, beside logs piled high ready for use. Around the walls in another room are pictures of the earliest types of cars, and of all sorts of other modes of transport. A dwelling house was on the site of the pub in 1060. Later, the building was the guest house for the nearby Benedictine priory. One previous tenant stayed on for 55 years, so it took a hold on her.

Much of the food here is home-made. The landlord's wife, an expert cook, specialises in pies. On a changing menu you might find lemon and coriander chicken, spicy orange pork, a half-pheasant casseroled in red wine, cheese and asparagus flan or home-cooked ham, both with salad and chips. To follow, you could have profiteroles or choose from a selection of gateaux, or opt for an apple crumble and cream like few other apple crumbles you've tasted. Real ales such as Adnams, Greene King and Tolly's are there for your enjoyment, as is Stowford Press.

The pub is open every day of the week, both at lunchtimes and in the evenings, for drinking and for meals. Children prepared to sit with their parents at table are welcome and they have a menu of their own. There is a garden for them to let off steam in. Dogs are permitted in the garden only, if well-behaved.

Telephone: 01986 785257.

How to get there: Go to Halesworth, which lies on the A144 Bungay to Darsham (A12) road. From the northern part of Halesworth take Wissett Road going north-west, through Wissett. Rumburgh will be reached in 4 miles. The inn is on the main road.

Parking: Beside the pub is a large car park.

Length of the walk: 2 miles or 3 miles. Map: OS Landranger sheet 156 Saxmundham, Aldeburgh and surrounding area (inn GR 345814).

At first the walk passes through the churchyard of St Michael's church. This is the site of an ancient Benedictine abbey which existed here until the time of the Reformation. Very little of the original abbey remains. After a long cross-field path, the walk continues on pleasant headland paths beside watercourses. There are good wide views to the north and east across this rich agricultural land.

The Walk

From the Rumburgh Buck go north along the road and in ¼ mile turn right along a gravel path towards St Michael's church. After crossing a small pasture enter the churchyard and pass the south porch of the church. Turn sharp right and leave the churchyard across a long, narrow footbridge. The route on the official map is half-left for a few yards through a shelter belt of young shrubs and small trees. Should the path be overgrown, skirt for 50 yards round the left-hand end of the shelter belt.

Now head straight across the field, roughly parallel to the boundary on the right, making for a point 10 to 20 yards to the left of an electricity pylon which appears behind the houses on the opposite side of the field. On the far side, at a wooden signpost, turn left along a well-used headland path, with a ditch on the right. At the corner of the field cross a ditch by a two-

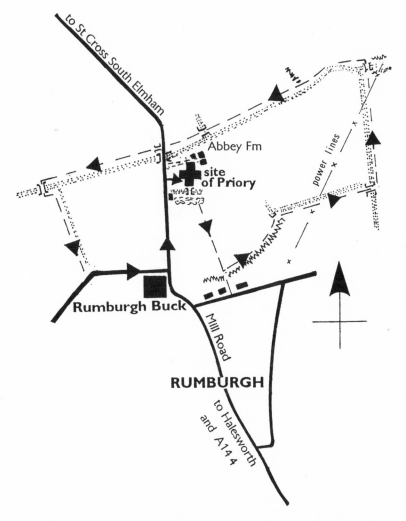

sleeper bridge and continue straight on, now with a ditch on the left.

Halfway across the field go under grid lines and at the far side cross a two-sleeper bridge and turn left along a headland beside a ditch on the left.

Soon after walking under the grid lines again, reach the corner of the field, and cross a two-sleeper bridge by two signposts. Here turn left, on a grassy headland path, beside a ditch with an occasional tree, on the left. Go through a cross-hedge and continue beside the ditch. Approaching the farm on the left, go across a wide cartbridge over another drainage ditch and

The church of St Michael and St Felix, Rumburgh.

continue, still with a ditch on the left, on a good headland path. Climb an embankment beside a bridge and cross some white railings out to a road.

For the shorter walk, you may return directly along the road to the Buck from this point, which is close to Rumburgh church.

For the main walk, cross the road and go down the bank beside the end of the bridge parapet and over a sleeper bridge. There is another footpath sign here. Follow a headland path beside a stream on the left.

At the corner of the field cross another sleeper bridge and continue, as before, on the headland for about 300 yards. Turn left and cross the stream on a long concrete bridge with a bent steel handrail. Turn left and go back for 20 yards on the opposite side of the stream, then turn right along a headland and follow a ditch on the left. After passing some barns, behind the hedge on the left, reach a narrow road.

Turn left and walk along the road, with a good view of the church, away half-left, back to the village street. The Rumburgh Buck is a few yards to the right.

Places of interest nearby

Wissett Vineyard offers tours of the vineyard and wine tasting by arrangement. Telephone: 01986 785216.

⑰ Orford
The Crown and Castle Hotel

Orford is on the estuary of the river Ore, beyond which lies Orford Spit, a 9-mile shingle bank, now owned by the National Trust, most of which is a nature reserve. In the late 1930s a secret research station to develop radar was built here. Nowadays, however, apart from the small town of Orford with its castle, the area is one of lonely seas and skies, and haunting marshes, where the only noise is likely to be the splash of an oar or a sea bird's cry.

A mere stone's throw from Orford Castle is the Crown and Castle Hotel. This very comfortable hostelry has several bars and a restaurant, grouped around a central serving area. On the walls are accounts of the uses to which the Orford Ness secret establishment was put. The hotel was one of the 'locals' for the boffins when they came ashore across the Alde.

Main courses to choose from include lasagne verdi, traditional beef steak and kidney pie, chicken Kiev, grilled sirloin steak, deep fried fish platter, grilled salmon steak, vegetable pasta bake, and how about swordfish with tomato and coriander sauce? If you are still hungry, there are sweets such as vanilla slice, Black Forest gateau and strawberry cheesecake. The real ales served here are Adnams, as befits an establishment so close to Adnams brewery at Southwold. Scrumpy Jack draught cider can be purchased too.

The hotel is open and meals are served at almost any time of day, from 11 am to 11 pm six days a week and all permitted hours on Sundays. Children are welcome, and have their own menu. Besides a family room there is a garden for them to play in, if you can tear them away from the castle. Dogs are allowed inside if well trained in social behaviour. Accommodation at the Crown and Castle is no problem, there is room for many guests. Telephone: 01394 450205.

How to get there: Turn off the A12 at the roundabout just north of Woodbridge, onto the A1152. Continue through Melton and in 2 miles where the main road forks left, keep straight on along the B1084 to Orford. At the square turn right to the pub at the far end of the square.

Parking: There is a fair-sized car park behind the hotel, some parking in the square, and lots more down towards the quay, opposite the Jolly Sailors. The castle car park may be used by people visiting the castle.

Length of the walk: 1 ¾ miles or 3 ¾ miles. Map: OS Landranger sheet 156 Saxmundham, Aldeburgh and surrounding area (inn GR 421499).

This easy walk is in two parts. The first is across the marshes to the river wall and the quay and back to the castle. The second section goes through the castle grounds and along cross-field paths and lanes around the farm land behind the town.

The Walk
From the Crown and Castle walk through the square towards St Bartholomew's church. Enter the churchyard, pass the south porch and swing right to leave by the gate on the south side at a road junction.

Walk straight on down the road opposite. Pass on the left a terrace of cottages and take the first road to the left. Pass on the left a narrow road. To the right, you can see Orford lighthouse, a white tower with two red bands, which stands on Orford Spit.

After passing a second road on the left and then a large cream-painted house behind a high brick wall, go right, opposite where the wall on the left ends, along a wide, grassy track through a pedestrian gate beside a large steel gate.

Continue beside a row of cupressus trees on the right and, where the trees end, keep straight on along the grassy cart track beside a ditch on the right, towards the lighthouse. At the point where the ditch turns left, cross it by a culvert and immediately turn half-right along a cross-field path towards steps up the flood protection wall, just over 100 yards away. After crossing a wide drainage ditch on a narrow path, climb the steps. At the top there is a

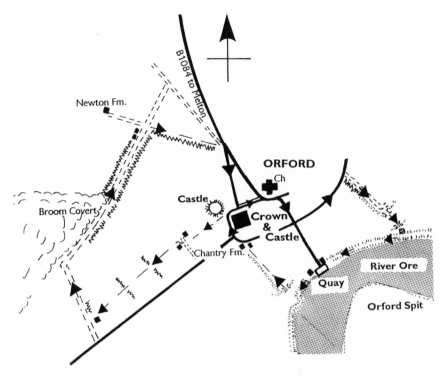

wide panorama of the river estuary and Orford Spit nature reserve. You can
see the buildings and aerials of the former research station.

Turn right along the river wall. Shortly cross a stile onto a narrow footpath
which leads past the Orford Sailing Club, then go left down the steps to
Orford quay.

Go straight over the quay, where boats leave for the Spit and for Havergate Island bird reserve, and continue on the tarmac path beside the water,
passing cream-washed Quay House on the right.

Go right through a squeezer stile and then climb the steps up the flood
bank. Turn left and walk along the top. Over to the right you can see the
castle, church and town of Orford. You come to a point about 300 yards
from the quay where the river wall makes a turn to the left and then a sharp
turn back again. Here drop down, half-right, off the wall, to cross a wide
ditch by a plank bridge which rather surprisingly is right against a newish
culverting of the ditch. Continue on a broad headland track beside a narrow
ditch on the left and at the end of a field cross a stile and walk towards the
castle. Soon go straight through the yard of Chantry Farm, turn left at the
road and almost immediately swing right.

Orford Castle.

Where the road gradually bends right towards the inn, turn left through an iron gate and enter the castle grounds. Continue straight on, passing the castle keep, about 50 yards away to the right, and the humps and hollows of its former defences.

Orford Castle was built in the 12th century to defend the coast, by Henry II, who also intended to drain some of the marshes and develop the port. The 20-sided keep is roofed over, and visitors may wander from floor to floor. When at the top there are superb views over the marshes, the river Alde, Orford Ness and beyond.

Continuing the walk, pass a lane off to the left. The wide grass path soon becomes a narrow path between a fence on the right and a hedge on the left. Go straight over a tarmac drive and then dog-leg right and left and continue straight ahead, first on a headland path then a cross-field path, making for a Dutch barn in the distance.

Continue on cross-field paths and then pass the Dutch barn on the left. Descend steps into a sunken lane and turn right onto a broad, flinty cart track which in ¼ mile, at the edge of a forest, turns half-right. The track widens, and the conifer plantation on the left gives way to a tall hedge. Pass on the left two pairs of cottages and then turn right, opposite the lane to Newton Farm on the left, to walk a well-used headland path, with a hedge on the right.

At the far side of the field turn right along a broad track, with the fire station behind the hedge on the left. Pass the primary school on the right, and bear round to the right along the road, which in 300 yards leads into the square, very close to the Crown and Castle.

Places of interest nearby

Orford Castle is open to the public daily from the start of April until the end of October from 10 am to 6 pm, and during November to the end of March it is open daily from 10 am to 4 pm. Occasionally there are special events such as falconry and Tudor entertainment. Telephone: 01394 450472. *Orford Museum*, round behind the Crown and Castle, is open every afternoon in summer from 2 pm to 4 pm. Birdwatchers can take a small boat down the river to land on *Havergate Island*, which belongs to the RSPB. Among the birds that nest there are avocets and short-eared owls. It is necessary to book your passage on this boat with the RSPB. Phone the RSPB shop (closed on Tuesdays) for details: 01728 648281.

18 Eastbridge
The Eel's Foot

Eastbridge is a small, isolated settlement on the edge of the broad area of marsh, lakes and meadows known as Minsmere. Much of this is the RSPB's prestigious bird reserve, extensive shallow wetlands. This is a grand place for both walkers and birdwatchers. The remote and lengthy coastline to the east has lent itself to smuggling. Around the middle of the 18th century smuggling was big business – hundreds and hundreds of farm carts, horses and smugglers at Sizewell Gap pitted their wits against the Government's Riding Officers, sometimes assisted by Dragoons. Often the officers were also in the pay of the smugglers.

The renowned Eel's Foot inn gives a friendly reception and it is a cheerful, snug place to be in. A roaring fire burns from early autumn onwards. The food is good and plentiful. On the changing menu, written on a labour-saving slatted blackboard, besides cod, scampi, savoury pie, steak and kidney, chicken pie, beefburger and sausage, all with chips and peas, there are quite a few vegetarian dishes, such as vegetable balti with naan bread, tikka masala and pilau rice, moussaka and quiche. An unusual, but popular, dish is kipper and a roll. Sweets on the menu include apple and sultana pudding, cherry pie and banana fudge cake. A variety of Adnams real ales are served, on a rotating basis. Scrumpy Jack draught cider is also on sale. Well-mannered children are welcome, and may sit in the lounge, to the right on entering the pub. They are catered for with either sausages or sea stars and chips. The garden is large, with a field beyond, and there is plenty of play apparatus. Well-behaved dogs are allowed in the bar.

The pub is open all day on Saturday, the permitted licensing hours on Sunday and at lunchtimes and in the evenings on Monday to Friday. No meals are served on Wednesday evenings. On Thursday evenings the pub puts on live music.

Telephone: 01728 830154.

How to get there: From the south, use the A12 and take the A1094 towards Aldeburgh. Turn left onto the B1069. Go straight through Leiston and ½ mile after passing the turning on the right to Sizewell, turn right on a minor road signed to Eastbridge. Eastbridge and the Eel's Foot are about one mile further. From the north take the B1122, Yoxford to Sizewell road. Go through Theberton and then turn left on a minor road signed to Eastbridge.

Parking: There is a large car park beside the pub. A chain is put across the entrance out of pub hours, but the landlord might let you leave the car there if you ask.

Length of the walk: 3½ miles. Map: OS Landranger sheet 156 Saxmundham, Aldeburgh and surrounding area (inn GR 452661).

After crossing the Minsmere river, in its shallow marshy valley, the walk climbs through silent and unspoilt mixed woodlands to a heather clad hill overlooking Middleton. It continues along a quiet access road to Minsmere bird reserve and then on a bridleway across another small hill where there are distant views of Sizewell, the sea and low-lying Minsmere, then returns through more woods to the Eel's Foot.

The Walk

Leave the Eel's Foot and turn right on a narrow road with willow trees planted on both sides. To the left you will see, across the meadows, overhead electricity wires with shuttle-shaped wire baskets threaded along the wires. These are markers to deter birds from colliding with the cables. It is only ¼ mile from the bird reserve.

Cross the New Cut of the Minsmere river and keep on the tarmac road. In ¼ mile pass Four Winds, a brick-built house with large wrought-iron entrance gates, beside which, hung on the gate pier, is a bell. Here, leave the tarmac road which bends right towards the bird reserve, and go straight on along a gravel track up through mixed woodlands with mature oaks, chestnut and larch. Keep on the track for a little under ½ mile until you

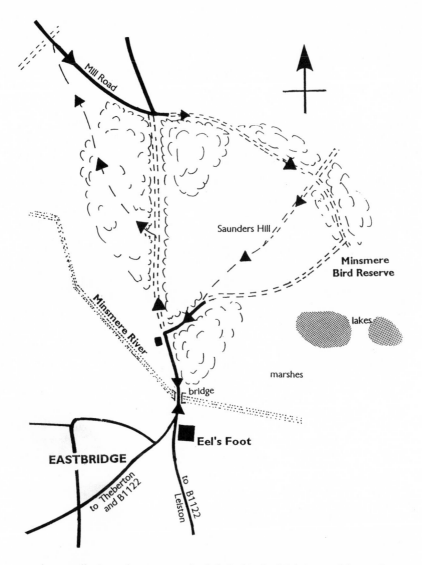

reach a small triangular area on the left, behind which is an old wooden gate beside a stile.

Cross the stile and follow a delightful grassy footpath through birch woods with occasional oaks and pine trees. Gradually, as the path climbs, the trees become fewer and there is more bracken. Eventually, you reach the top of the hill where the bracken has given way to heather and gorse. There are wide views to the left.

Minsmere river.

Go over a stile and continue beside gorse bushes on the left and an open field on the right. Pass a short length of rough timber fence on the left and then continue between tall gorse bushes, dropping down to meet a road which comes in obliquely from the right.

Turn right, making what is almost a U-turn. Walk along the narrow road – there is not much traffic. In ½ mile reach a junction where a tarmac road goes left and a cart track goes right. Go straight on along the tarmac road towards the Minsmere bird reserve. Pass on the left a smart brick bungalow behind a row of lime trees and continue between birch woods.

In 300 yards, where the road makes a slight bend to the right, the woods on the right end and a high hedge continues on the right. Further on, the road makes another slight bend to the right, close to a small sign giving details about visiting the RSPB reserve. At this point turn right onto a broad, grassy track up a hill, following a line of electricity poles. As you get to the top of the rise, looking half-left you will see the huge concrete cube and concrete dome of the Sizewell Generating Station, 3 miles away. Closer, and more to the left, the wetlands of Minsmere are just visible.

Keep to the track as it descends, getting narrower, through woods of hawthorn, oak and pine, to reach a tarmac road coming in from the left. Go straight on along the road between the woods.

The road bears left, passing the house, Four Winds, again. Continue back to the Eel's Foot and the start.

Places of interest nearby

Covering about 1,500 acres, the *Minsmere RSPB reserve* has many artificially made islands in it to encourage the breeding of birds such as avocets, which returned to the area during World War II, when the Minsmere levels were flooded for coastal protection against the enemy. Marsh harriers now breed on the reserve, as well as many other species. Telephone: 01728 648281. *Dunwich Heath* (**National Trust**) is close by, and two public hides by the shore, overlooking Minsmere, are easily reached from there. *Leiston Abbey* ruins are about 2½ miles away. The site is open to the public. *Sizewell Visitors' Centre*, next door to Sizewell Power Station, houses a fascinating permanent exhibition about every aspect of electricity generation, not just nuclear power. Free, and open every day except Christmas and New Year bank holidays. Telephone: 01728 642139.

⑲ Barnby
The Swan Inn

Barnby, with its twin village of North Cove, lies just at the edge of the Waveney marshes. The river Waveney, which forms the border between Suffolk and Norfolk, flows here within a mile-wide strip of flat, marshy land, isolated and lonely with few, if any, dwellings. It is criss-crossed with an intricate network of drainage ditches and the fields are grazed by cattle. However, much of the area is a nature reserve. Birds nest in the long grass and alongside the ditches. The Waveney is a navigable waterway which forms part of the extensive network of lakes and rivers comprising the Norfolk Broads.

The Swan is a popular pub, with several eating areas as well as a restaurant. A pale blue carpet complements the blue upholstery, and brass fire irons gleam beside a brass fender round the fireplace. In the restaurant the centrepiece is a wheelhouse from some small craft, in which sits, immobile, an old sailor, à la Madame Tussaud's. A ship's binnacle in working order, which can be lit up, takes pride of place in one bar and many charts and indentures, on parchment, are framed on the walls. Tables are placed outside for warm days.

On the menu are lots of fish dishes, such as prawn and lobster thermidor, brill fillet in a cheese and prawn sauce, fresh salmon with prawn and tarragon butter, whole grilled North Sea turbot or lemon sole, wing of skate in black butter, cod or plaice mornay and grilled sea bass fillets – the pub is owned by Lowestoft fish merchants. But if you insist on not having fish there is also fillet, sirloin or rump steak. A variety of sweets are listed to tempt you. Examples are banana split, meringue glacé chocolate nut sundae, pecan and maple pie and the amazing Swan Extravaganza. The ales on sale are Greene King Abbot, Adnams, Whitbread and one guest ale. Strongbow draught cider is also on offer. Meals are served seven days a week, both lunches and evening meals. The usual opening hours apply. Children are very welcome, and they may have half portions from the menu. There is a garden where they may play. Dogs are not allowed in the pub.

Telephone: 01502 476646.

How to get there: Barnby is about 5 miles from Beccles beside the A146 Lowestoft road. Barnby and North Cove are bypassed by the A146, so observe the signs to the village. The Swan is at the north-east end of Barnby, close to the A146.

Parking: There is a good car park at the Swan. Elsewhere, parking is limited to a few roadside spaces.

Length of the walk: 3½ miles. Maps: OS Landranger sheets 134 Norwich and The Broads and 156 Saxmundham, Aldeburgh and surrounding area (inn GR 477899).

This easy and pleasant walk uses country lanes with little traffic, cart tracks and well-trod footpaths, to cross the flat marshes to the bank of the Waveney. In summer the river is a busy waterway where cruisers and sailing craft go to and from Beccles, which is one of the terminal points of the Norfolk Broads. In contrast, winter sees few boats. The marshes, the watermeadows and the river then become a quiet haunt and breeding ground for many waterfowl and other wildlife.

The Walk

From The Swan go left along the green, passing a phone box, and in 100 yards turn left at a road junction.

Continue along the narrow, winding road, which does not carry much traffic. Pass, on the left, a pond. The road runs through light woodland for much of its way. Just over ½ mile from the Swan, and at a sharp right-hand bend, pass a track to the left to Fairfield Farm, a tall, yellow-painted, brown-roofed building. There is a footpath sign here.

About 100 yards beyond the lane to the farm, turn right at a footpath sign along a cart track towards a steel-gated railway crossing. Cross the railway, being careful to shut the gate, and continue on the lane through woods of

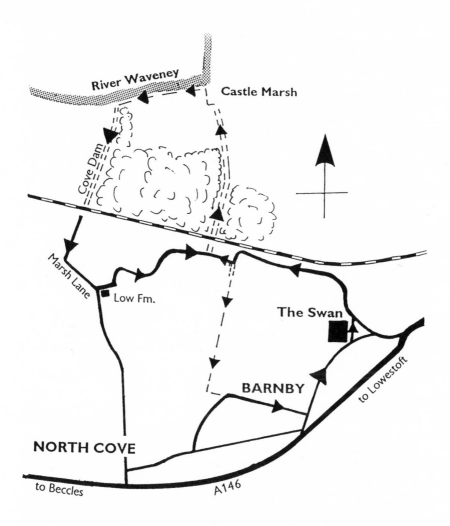

willow and alder. In 200 yards the woods on the right end and the lane continues, with a marshy field on the right. Shortly, there are fields on both sides of the lane.

At the end of the lane, close to a sign about the Castle Marsh nature reserve, cross a stile into grassland and go straight ahead to another stile just in front of some trees. Climb the bank, just beyond the stile, and turn left. You have now reached the bank of the river Waveney, which can be seen in a few yards. Follow the riverside path. In summer you will probably be walking alongside many small pleasure craft.

River Waveney near Barnby.

In about ¼ mile there is a sign beside the river about the fishing rights of the local angling club. Here, go left off the river bank and over a sleeper cartbridge, on a well-used track with grass in the middle. Cross the railway by a small pedestrian gate beside a level crossing. Continue along a narrow tarmac road. The road makes a sharp bend to the left and then at a three-way road junction you bear left towards Barnby.

Walk along the road. In about a mile and after several bends, reach the track off to the left, which was used earlier in the walk on the way to the river bank. Keep along the road for a further 100 yards and, where it bends sharply left, take the farm drive to the right towards Fairfield Farm. Do not swing right to the building or left, but keep straight on, with a hedge on the right. Go through a gap in a cross-hedge into the next field and continue on a narrow, well-used path between a hedge on the right and a fence on the left.

At the end of the field, the path turns left and runs into a narrow lane. Cross a stream by a concrete bridge and pass between two houses to come out to a road.

Go left along the road and then swing half-right. Pass School Close on the right and, after passing the modern development of Mill Way on the left, reach a T-junction. Turn left along the road to reach the Swan in about ¼ mile.

Walberswick

The Bell Hotel

This tranquil, quiet area can absorb a lot of people without in any way appearing crowded, as there are miles of beaches, river frontage and walks in the surrounding country to scatter visitors far and wide. It is an unspoilt area, no buses, no pavements, no street lights even – just quiet enjoyment of the natural environment.

The 600-year old Bell inn, so near to the shore and so near to the green, appears to be the focus of village life. It is a rambling, busy pub, with a succession of small, intimate areas and comfortable settles aplenty. Roaring log fires are a feature in winter. Where else have you seen gleaming, polished brass coal scuttles used as lampshades? From the windows you can look over the river Blyth across to Southwold. The pub has some accommodation. Walberswick is a place to linger in.

The food served is mainly home-cooked, for example quiche, various raised pies, roast beef, chicken and chips and Cromer crabs in season. A selection of sweets tempt you, including a delicious apple pie and cream. The evening menu offers such dishes as sugar-baked Suffolk ham with spiced peaches, duck à l'orange, The Bell fisherman's pie, fillet steak garni and T-bone steak. The pub serves Adnams Bitter, Extra and Broadside and, in winter, Adnams Old. Strongbow cider is also on sale.

The Bell is open all day six days a week and the permitted hours on Sundays. Meals are served every day at the usual hours, but not on Sunday evenings. Dogs are allowed in, if well-behaved. Children are welcome everywhere except in the lounge bar. The pub has a garden area, but most youngsters will want to play on the beach or by the river, crabbing maybe. Every year the British Crabbing Federation, formed at the Bell some years ago, both to amuse the children and to raise money for local charities, holds the National Crabbing Championships here in the summer holidays. Crabbing entails no cruelty as the greedy crabs merely cling to the bait as they are gently lifted into a bucket. Even the smallest child is sure to catch one.

Telephone: 01502 723109.

How to get there: Use the A12 Ipswich to Lowestoft road. Turn off at Toby's Walks picnic site on the B1387, and keep straight on to Walberswick. The Bell is on the right 200 yards beyond the green.

Parking: The County Council have provided two large car parks close to the beach.

Length of the walk: 2½ miles. Map: OS Landranger sheet 156 Saxmundham, Aldeburgh and surrounding area (inn GR 499747).

This pleasant and easy walk starts along the bank of the river Blyth where, in summer, a rowing boat will ferry passengers across to Southwold. It continues beside Southwold harbour, passing many craft moored at tiny timber jetties on both sides. The walk then follows a cycle track along the route of the former light railway, which ran between Southwold and Halesworth, and then crosses Walberswick Common, back to the village. The scenery changes for the final part of the walk, which, after crossing the tidal Dunwich river and a narrow strip of marsh, reaches the North Sea. The return is along the shore, an excellent place for kite-flying.

The Walk

From the Bell go to the road, turn right and continue to just beyond the last house on the left. Here go left at the footpath sign before the car park. Walk alongside the garden wall of Old Vicarage Cottage at first, then swing right along a paving slab path on a raised bank.

When you reach the river go left to follow the river wall for about ½ mile. To your right is Southwold and to your left you can see Walberswick church.

At a path junction, with a Bailey bridge on your right, go left on a surfaced track. Follow this track as it later bends left by a memorial seat. When you almost reach some houses on the right, and within sight of a terrace of houses at right angles to the road, go left on a grassy path, just by a slender electricity pole bearing a 'Neighbourhood Watch' sign.

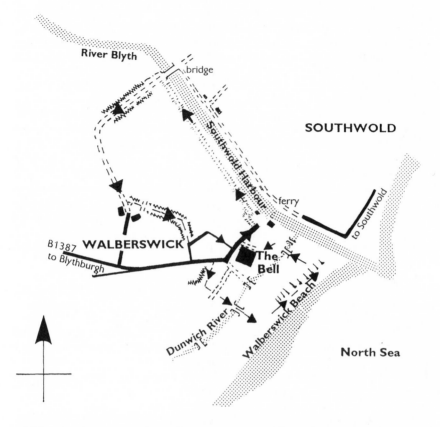

River Blyth

bridge

SOUTHWOLD

Southwold Harbour

ferry

to Southwold

B1387 **WALBERSWICK**
to Blythburgh

The
Bell

Walberswick Beach

Dunwich River

North Sea

Make a scissors crossing of a grassy cart track and carry on along a footpath. Pass a cart track leading from your right into a field on your left and keep on along an earth track between hedges. Soon you join a minor road, on a bend, with a thatched, pink house opposite. Turn left and follow this road until you reach the green. Keep right, join the road, and swing right past the village's seat, with its thatched roof, and walk as far as the Anchor public house.

Immediately before the Anchor turn left off the road onto a track. When the track swings left you keep straight on, passing a smart pair of wooden farm gates, with a hedge on the right. When that hedge goes right, at a skew T-junction, go left, heading towards the dunes. Meet a rough track, snake left and quickly right, cross the Dunwich river on a wooden footbridge and go ahead to climb the shingle bank to see the North Sea.

Go left along the shore, the relentless waves beating on the shingle, until you come to the second red lifebelt stand. Here turn inland, back over the

View of Southwold across the Blyth from Walberswick.

dunes and briefly over the marshes, to a gravelly track and another foot-bridge over the Dunwich river.

Cross the beach car park, bear left to some concrete steps, go up and over the flood wall, and walk back to the flag-topped Bell.

Places of interest nearby

The church of St Andrew, Walberswick, with the adjacent ruins of an earlier church, is on the road to Blythburgh. The church tower is far older than the church in use today, and is even older than the ruins alongside it.